ELIZABETH GASKELL

Women Writers

General Editors: *Eva Figes* and *Adele King*

Published titles

Forthcoming

Women Writers

Elizabeth Gaskell

Jane Spencer

St. Martin's Press   New York

© Jane Spencer 1993

First published in the United States of America in 1993

Printed in Hong Kong

ISBN 0–312–06058–0

Library of Congress Cataloging-in-Publication Data
Spencer, Jane.
Elizabeth Gaskell / Jane Spencer.
p.   cm.—(Women writers)
ISBN 0–312–06058–0
1. Gaskell, Elizabeth Cleghorn, 1810–1865—Criticism and
interpretation. 2. Women and literature—England—
History—19th century. I. Title. II. Series.
PR4711.S67 1993
823'.8—dc20
                                                          92–30539
                                                          CIP

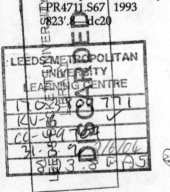

Contents

Acknowledgements

An earlier version of chapter 2 appeared in *The Gaskell Society Journal*, vol. 2, 1988, as '*Mary Barton* and Thomas Carlyle'. I am grateful to the editor, Alan Shelston, for permission to use the material here. I would also like to thank John Chapple and Arthur Pollard, the editors of *The Letters of Mrs Gaskell*, and Manchester University Press, the publishers, for permission to quote from their edition.

Thanks go to Ian Campbell, Gareth Roberts, Peter Keating, and Valerie Shaw, who helped me at various times by discussing Gaskell with me, and especially to Josephine McDonagh, who read and commented on chapters in draft. I would also like to thank all the students who took the special option on Elizabeth Gaskell in Edinburgh in the years 1985–7, and those who took the 'Women's Writing' option in Exeter in the years 1989–92. Their stimulating discussions of Gaskell helped me enormously.

I am very grateful to Marion Shaw and Patsy Stoneman, whose course 'Women in Literature and Society' first introduced me to Gaskell, and to much else.

Thanks to Hugh and Kate, for being there.

JANE SPENCER

Editors' Preface

The study of women's writing has been long neglected by a male critical establishment both in academic circles and beyond. As a result, many women writers have either been unfairly neglected or have been marginalised in some way, so that their true influence and importance has been ignored. Other women writers have been accepted by male critics and academics, but on terms which seem, to many women readers of this generation, to be false or simplistic. In the past the internal conflicts involved in being a woman in a male-dominated society have been largely ignored by readers of both sexes, and this has affected our reading of women's work. The time has come for a serious reassessment of women's writing in the light of what we understand today.

This series is designed to help in that reassessment.

All the books are written by women because we believe that men's understanding of feminist critique is only, at best, partial. And besides, men have held the floor quite long enough.

EVA FIGES
ADELE KING

Notes on the Texts

1 Warring Members: Elizabeth Gaskell, Writer

There are many Elizabeth Gaskells. She has been described as a sweet, gentle, utterly conventional Victorian woman who happened unawares to write some good novels; and as supporter of the women's movement whose writing embodies a rational and radical social critique.[1] In her lifetime much of her work was controversial: *Mary Barton* brought accusations from the manufacturers that she was too much on the side of the workers; the first volume of *Ruth* was burnt by some respectable men of her acquaintance; and the first edition of *The Life of Charlotte Brontë* had to be withdrawn because of threatened libel action. Yet by the early years of the twentieth century many of her readers thought of her chiefly as the charming author of delightful *Cranford*. Reviving interest in Gaskell from the 1950s onwards has reopened old controversies and started new ones. Marxist critics, reassessing her novels of industrial life, have praised her sympathetic rendering of working-class life, but concluded that she was an apologist for middle-class power.[2] Feminist critics re-reading her presentation of gender relations have found her on the contrary deeply critical of the power structures of her society.[3]

Such widely disparate assessments reflect inevitable differences among readers approaching a writer in different contexts and from different points of view; but the proliferation of Elizabeth Gaskells is not entirely the responsibility of her critics. She, herself, felt split, and not simply into two but into a multiplicity of selves whose warring allegiances were hard to disentangle. In 1850, when she moved with her family – her husband William, minister of the Unitarian Cross Street Chapel in Manchester, and their four daughters – to a large house in Plymouth Grove, feelings of guilt prompted her to express a dizzying sense of self-fragmentation. She wrote to a friend, the artist Eliza Fox, about the new house:

> You *must* come and see us in it, dearest Tottie, and try and make me see 'the wrong the better cause,' and that it is right to spend so much ourselves on *so* purely selfish a thing as a house is, while so many are wanting – thats the haunting thought to me; at least to one of my 'Mes,' for I have a great number, and that's the plague. One of my mes is, I do believe, a true Christian – (only people call her socialist and communist), another of my mes is a wife and mother, and highly delighted at the delight of everyone else in the house, Meta and William most especially who are in full extasy. Now that's my 'social' self I suppose. Then again I've another self with a full taste for beauty and convenience wh[ic]h is pleased on its own account. How am I to reconcile all these warring members? I try to drown myself (my *first* self,) by saying it's W[illia]m who is to decide on all these things, and his feeling it right ought to be my rule, And so it is – only that does not quite do. Well! I must try and make the house give as much pleasure to others as I can and make it as little selfish a thing as I can. My dear! its 150 a year, and I dare say we shall be ruined ... (*L* 108)

Gaskell's 'first', Christian self is clearly the self that has played a large part in writing *Mary Barton*, her first novel, published a year and a half before this, and earning her the name 'communist' from some readers. This self is haunted by thoughts of the 'wanting' workers of Manchester, with whom she has tried to unite in sympathy in her writing, but whose separation from her is underlined and increased by the move to Plymouth Grove. Another self, the family woman, is invoked to dispel guilt, but only raises another troubling question – the problem of how far a woman should be absorbed in husband and children. (Interestingly, it is the wife and mother Gaskell calls her 'social' self, rather than the self that is more concerned with the society beyond her family.) Two perceived duties, the wife's and the Christian's, clash; and this means that either can take on – temporarily, by way of contrast with the other – an aspect of indulgence. The first, conscience-stricken self has a status independent of husband and family, and is a writer. Yet the projected drowning of that self in William's guidance is not quite the suicidal act suggested by the imagery, because there are other, less conscientious selves ready to benefit from the death of the first; not only the wife and mother enjoying others' joy but an independent self 'pleased on its own account', whose 'taste for beauty' is also crucial to Gaskell the writer. 'Only that does not quite do': because Gaskell cannot accept the traditional subordination of wife to husband, or because she cannot allow herself the pleasures that relationship authorises here? Unable to turn her warring parts into a unified self, Gaskell turns from self altogether towards the end of the passage, aiming to quiet conscience by making her wealth into something for others. This move outwards from the divided self is one she makes many times in her writing.

1850 seems to have been a year in which Gaskell took stock of her life as a woman (approaching forty, with a family of girls, the eldest of them reaching marriage-able age) and as an author (who had been writing for years but had only recently become a public figure). In another letter written to Eliza Fox during this year the theme of the split self is related to the dilemma facing women artists. Gaskell writes to her friend of the problem troubling them both:

> about home duties and individual life; it is just my puzzle; and I don't think I can get nearer to a solution than you have done. . . . One thing is pretty clear, *Women*, must give up living an artist's life, if home duties are to be paramount. It is different with men, whose home duties are so small a part of their life. However we are talking of women. I am sure it is healthy for them to have the refuge of the hidden world of Art to shelter themselves in when too much pressed upon by daily small Lilliputian arrows of peddling cares; it keeps them from being morbid as you say; and takes them into the land where King Arthur lies hidden, and soothes them with its peace. I have felt this in writing, I see others feel it in music, you in painting, so assuredly a blending of the two is desirable. (Home duties and the development of the Individual I mean), which you will say it takes no Solomon to tell you but the difficulty is where and when to make one set of duties subserve and give place to the other. (*L* 106)

Because, in this formulation, a woman's domestic duties are implicitly identified with the real world, individual development through art becomes not a genuine alternative to them, but merely a delightful, temporary escape into a misty Arthurian world of legend and faery. In keeping with this view of art's escapist function, Gaskell was later to find some of her own works soothing refuges from reality: *Cranford*, for example, was a book she loved to re-read for amusement when she was ill or tired. Escaping from home duties always meant, for her, escaping from Manchester too, and the countryside represented a refuge intimately bound up with art's power of enchantment. On one occasion she wrote of a visit to Shottery, near Stratford-upon-Avon,

> the rural inhabitants . . . believed in ghosts, and told some capital stories thereupon; . . . and we had brilliantly fine days when we went long drives; in one of which (to a place where I believed the Sleeping Beauty lived, it was so over-grown and hidden up by woods) I SAW a ghost! Yes I did. (*L* 81)

The countryside, countrymen's beliefs, ghosts, fairies, the Sleeping Beauty and King Arthur all came together, for Gaskell, in the stories people told and the stories she told herself: they made up her hidden world of Art.

Art so viewed was a self-indulgence, justifiable only for its therapeutic value as it restored a tired and harassed family woman cheerfully to her duties. Gaskell's commitment to her writing could neither be explained nor justified by this alone. She laid her letter on home duties and the individual on one side for a day or two and returned to it with a very different view of the artist's role:

> If Self is to be the end of exertions, those exertions are unholy, there is no doubt of *that* – and that is part of the danger in cultivating the Individual Life; but I do believe we have all some appointed work to do, wh[ic]h no one else can do so well; Wh[ich] is *our* work; what *we* have to do in advancing the Kingdom of God; and that first we must find out what we are

sent into the world to do, and define it and make it clear to ourselves, (that's *the* hard part) and then forget ourselves in our work, and our work in the End we ought to strive to bring about. (*L* 107)

This time art appears not as an escape from the world but as a religious mission within it. It was this view that could most easily serve to justify a woman's dedication to art. Instead of fleeing from her home duties by writing she could see herself as fulfilling them, once they were reinterpreted (in a way that Christian belief allowed them to be) as duties to the entire community, not just to her own husband and children. In her attempt to heal the troubling split between woman and writer, then, Gaskell, echoing a typical preoccupation of Victorian aesthetics, developed a split view of art's function – art as escape, versus art as service.

For all the contradictory feelings reported in these letters of 1850, Gaskell's different 'mes', with their various commitments, ended up producing an important body of literary work. The five full-length novels, plus the difficult-to-classify *Cranford*, a major biography and over thirty stories, are ample evidence that the clash of 'these warring members' of the self issued in the production of Elizabeth Gaskell the writer.

She was born Elizabeth Cleghorn Stevenson on 29 September 1810, the eighth child of Elizabeth Holland and William Stevenson, but only the second to survive infancy – the other was her brother John, twelve years her senior. William Stevenson had been a Unitarian minister, then an experimental farmer and a journalist before moving to London as Keeper of Records at the Treasury. Elizabeth Holland was also a Unitarian, whose father Samuel combined farming and preaching like Holman in 'Cousin Phillis'. The importance of the future writer's religious background can hardly be overstated. Unitarians had been one of the Dissenting groups in the eighteenth century; they were subject to civil disabilities and even, in theory, to imprisonment, because they denied the divinity of Christ and the existence of the Trinity. After the Trinity Bill of 1813 repealed old statutes that told against it, the sect expanded in a climate of greater toleration, and became a powerful social group, with members in the professions, in Parliament, and in movements for social reform; and Elizabeth Gaskell was to number many prominent Unitarian families among her friends. Still she remained aware of prejudice against her from some orthodox believers, and when Charlotte Brontë married a curate Gaskell was 'terribly afraid he won't let her go on being as intimate with us, heretics' (L 280). The 'heretics' held that the truths of religion were to be sought through reason rather than scriptural authority, and stressed the importance of Christian charity, tolerance for all shades of belief, and concern for social welfare. Elizabeth Gaskell's character and writing were profoundly affected by this most broad-minded of religious sects. Her Unitarian convictions lie behind the religious and didactic tone of much of her writing, and equally inform the unorthodox content of its message. They show in her (somewhat ambiguous) championship of the working class in *Mary Barton*; in her concern with outcasts from respectable society like the unmarried mother of *Ruth*; in her recurrent suspicion of authority in Church or State, and in her constant message of tolerance and reconciliation wherever people were divided by belief, class or the barriers of social disgrace. One scene from *North and South* captures the essence of her hope for bringing opposing groups together – the central theme of this novel, perhaps of all her work. Bessy Higgins is dead and her father, despite his atheism, agrees to join the Hales in family prayer. 'Margaret the Churchwoman, her father the Dissenter, Higgins the Infidel, knelt down together. It did them no harm' (*NS* 297).

It was mainly through her mother's family that the young Elizabeth Stevenson's religious and social outlook was formed. She was only thirteen months old when her mother died, and her mother's sister offered to look after her. In 1811 Elizabeth was taken to the home of her 'dear aunt Lumb' in Knutsford, Cheshire, a small country town sixteen miles from Manchester. Her happy childhood there inspired the affectionate and nostalgic pictures of country life in *Wives and Daughters*, where Hollingford is reminiscent of the Cheshire town, and most famously, in *Cranford*.

In 1814, William Stevenson remarried. Elizabeth saw little of her new stepmother and disliked what she did see.[4] In 1822 she was sent to the Miss Byerleys' school in Barford, Warwickshire (it was moved to Stratford-upon-Avon in 1824). The school offered a more liberal education than most girls' schools of the time, and Elizabeth spent five happy years there.[5] As her schooldays ended, a period of family troubles began. Her brother John, who was in the merchant navy, went missing on a voyage to India in 1828–9. The family never found out what had happened to him. This loss, which affected his sister deeply, was followed soon afterwards by William Stevenson's death in 1829.

After her father's death Elizabeth spent some time on visits to various relatives and friends. It was while visiting Manchester with Anne Turner in 1831 that she met William Gaskell, then assistant minister (and later the minister) at the Unitarian Cross Street Chapel. They soon became engaged, and married in 1832. After a honeymoon in North Wales Elizabeth Gaskell began the busy Manchester life which she found so fulfilling, exhausting and difficult. She soon became pregnant, and her first child, a daughter, was stillborn the year after her marriage. In 1834, her first living child, Marianne, was born, followed by another daughter, Meta, in 1837. In addition to running the household and caring for the children, Gaskell undertook other work that was an extension of her wifely role: she taught in the Sunday School, did good works among the congregation, and helped her husband in his literary work. Besides his Cross Street work William Gaskell was a lecturer, teaching at various times at Manchester New College and at the Mechanics' Institute for working-class men. The Gaskells' collaboration on literary ventures such as William's lectures on the English poets was especially important to Elizabeth. She perhaps originally expected her marriage to provide a shared literary vocation. She told Mary Howitt in 1838, 'We once thought of *trying* to write sketches among the poor, *rather* in the manner of Crabbe . . . but in a more seeing-beauty spirit; and one – the only one – was published in *Blackwood*, January 1837.' She added rather plaintively, 'But I suppose we spoke of our plan near a dog-rose, for it never went any further' (*L* 33).

In fact, as her husband became more absorbed in his work and life in the smoke and dirt and among the poverty of Manchester began to oppress her spirits, Gaskell was coming to regard literature and the countryside together as escapes from her everyday life. A country holiday was always necessary to her after emotional trauma – a trip to North Wales, for example, helped her recover from the blow of aunt Lumb's death soon after Meta's birth – and her correspondence with Mary Howitt shows how reading could be a substitute escape when a journey was impossible. In spring, she longed

> to be off into the deep grassy solitudes of the country . . . But as I happen to be a woman instead of a bird, as I have ties at home and duties to perform . . . why I must stay at home and content myself with recalling the happy scenes which your books bring up before me. (*L* 14)

If the world of literature offered an escape, though, it also provided a way of confronting the harshness of the existence around her, and her early stories are as concerned with revealing social realities as they are with offering enchantment. The two strands were to be interwoven in all her work.

By writing to Mary Howitt, the writer of several articles in literary journals, Gaskell was probably feeling her way to getting some of her own work published. Her diary about her daughters tails off in 1838; possibly she was now using her writing time for stories. Her correspondence with the Howitts led to friendship and to the beginnings of her writing career. Her essay on Clopton Hall (based on a visit during her schooldays) was included in William Howitt's *Visits to Remarkable Places* in 1840, and later she published stories in his *Howitt's Journal*.

As Gaskell made tentative steps towards her writing vocation, her family increased. One of her letters refers to a son who died in infancy some time between Meta's birth and the birth of another daughter, Florence, in 1842.[6] A second son, Willie, was born in 1844. In the summer of 1845 Willie, aged ten months, died of scarlet fever. 'That wound will never heal on earth, although hardly any one knows how it has changed me', she wrote three years later (*L* 57). One of the changes precipitated, if not caused, by her loss was her transformation from an occasional writer to a professional novelist. She began writing a full-length work of fiction as a way of working through her grief, and *Mary Barton* was the result. Gaskell, always the enemy of self-centredness, wrote not to express her own grief but on behalf of others who suffered – the workers of Manchester, whose poverty had distressed her. Her personal loss is touched on in the preface, and surfaces in the novel in the repeated motif of a son's death. Meanwhile, Willie's loss was followed by the birth of another daughter, Julia, in 1846. *Mary Barton* was finished in the following year, and William Howitt showed it on Gaskell's behalf to John Forster, a reader for the publishing house Chapman and Hall. They accepted it, paid £100 for the copyright, and published the novel late in 1848.

Mary Barton soon became a great publishing success and a source of controversy. Published in the year of European revolutions and dealing with a workers' strike in the Manchester of the 'hungry forties', it made a Carlylean attack on the *laissez-faire* philosophy of political economists, and insisted that the rich should recognise that their responsibilities to the poor went beyond paying them their low wages. To some working-class readers, Gaskell was a champion of their cause for presenting their lives realistically and sympathetically, while some part of her middle-class audience was moved by her appeal to their consciences. Although Gaskell protested that she had no intention of setting class against class, many readers interpreted her novel as supporting the workers against capitalist management, and she was bound to anger the manufacturers of Manchester, who felt threatened by her revelation of the appalling conditions in which their workforce lived. Some of the strongest opposition came from the Gaskells' own acquaintances. W. R. Greg criticised her in the *Edinburgh Review* for suggesting that employers were to blame for poverty, and argued that hard work and thrift, without any wage increases, would be enough to make the mill workers prosperous.[7] Not all employers, though, opposed all interference with market forces, and Gaskell reported that 'Half the masters here are bitterly angry with me – half (and the best half) are buying it to give to their work-people's libraries'. She added 'I had no idea it would have proved such a fire brand' (*L* 68).

Although her novel was published anonymously, and Gaskell remained for some time reluctant to own it publicly, the secret of her authorship was soon out, and when she visited London in the spring of 1849 she was lionised. From this time on, it was clear that authorship had transformed her life. She made many new friends and acquaintances in literary circles, including Dickens, Carlyle and Charlotte Brontë. She began to travel more widely and often, usually with one or more of her daughters, rarely with her husband, who was tied to his Manchester work. Trips abroad, to Heidelberg, Paris and Rome, became frequent in her later years. They gave her the breaks from home she needed to concentrate on work in progress or to recover from completing a project, and they were financed by work already sold. Literature, the solace of her imagination, began to provide her with a literal escape from domestic life.

Gaskell's somewhat uneasy friendship with Dickens was of great importance to her writing. He asked her to write for *Household Words*, and in 1850 she began her career as his 'Scheherezade', contributing numerous stories and two longer works, *Cranford* (1851–3) and *North and South* (1854–5) to the periodical. Later she wrote for its successor, *All the Year Round*.

Cranford began as a couple of papers for *Household Words*. Dickens greeted it with delight, and it was eventually expanded into a full-length work. Its humorous pictures of a country community came as a kind of light relief after her first novel, but Gaskell was soon returning to more controversial territory. In her next novel, *Ruth* (1853), she tackled the thorny subject of society's typical ostracism of unmarried mothers, once again challenging her contemporaries to put into practice the religious values they professed to hold. After her experience with *Mary Barton* she was well aware that she would provoke hostile reactions with *Ruth*, and she looked forward to its appearance with dread, complaining, 'I hate publishing because of the talk people make' (*L* 209).

Not long after *Ruth*'s appearance Gaskell was planning another novel: a return to the subject of industrial capitalism, in which she hoped, by giving more consideration to the manufacturers' viewpoint, to avoid the controversy that had surrounded her first novel. *North and South* brought her problems of a different kind, though. She sent Dickens a proposal for a full-length work in 1853, and it was planned to bring it out in weekly instalments in 1854. Dickens wanted short chapters ending on a note of suspense, and Gaskell provided the slow development of a complex theme which needed to be presented in larger units. Sales of *Household Words* began to drop after a few weeks of Gaskell's serial, but she was reluctant to alter her work to fit the magazine's requirements. By the end of 1854 she was 'sick of writing': her novel, she complained, 'has been a terrible weight on me and has made me have some of the most felling headaches I ever had in my life' (*L* 325). She always remained dissatisfied with its 'huddled' ending.

The fruitful and stressful years that followed the publication of *Mary Barton* also saw the development of a friendship that would lead the novelist to turn biographer, and produce her most controversial work

of all. In the summer of 1850, while staying in the Lake
District with Sir James and Lady Kay-Shuttleworth,
Gaskell met Charlotte Brontë. At this time Brontë's
fame, as the author of *Jane Eyre* and *Shirley*, was
spreading, while her personal life was made acutely
miserable by the swiftly successive losses of her brother
Branwell and her sisters Emily and Anne. Gaskell was
fascinated by Brontë the victim of misfortune as much
as by Brontë the artist.

> She is the last of six; lives in a wild out of the way
> village in the Yorkshire Moors with a wayward
> eccentric wild father, – their parsonage facing the
> North – no flowers or shrub or tree can grow in the
> plot of ground, on acc[oun]t of the biting winds. . . .
> Indeed I never heard of so hard, and dreary a life.
>
> (*L* 128)

The two writers became friends, and Gaskell invited
Brontë to stay, hoping to impart some family warmth
into her cold and lonely life. From first to last her
feelings towards the younger writer were of motherly
protectiveness – with a touch of motherly condescension – towards this 'little lady in a black silk gown'
(*L* 123). Brontë did eventually visit the Gaskells, and
their friendship continued through correspondence; but
as she had feared, Gaskell heard rather less of her
friend after her marriage to Arthur Nicholls, and she
did not hear of Brontë's illness until she heard of her
death in April 1855. Her grief was sharpened by her
feeling that she might have been able to prevent it:
'How I wish I had known! . . . I do fancy that if I had
come, I could have induced her . . . to do what was
absolutely necessary, for her very life' (*L* 337). She very

soon began gathering materials for a biography, which she saw as her chance to do what she could for the memory of a woman she had been unable to help as she wanted to in life.

The Life of Charlotte Brontë was published early in 1857, and Gaskell, in need of a holiday after two years' intense and emotionally exhausting work, went to Rome with her daughters at the time the work came out. During her six weeks there she established a deep friendship with Charles Eliot Norton, later an art historian, with whom she corresponded during the rest of her life. 'It was in those charming Roman days that my life, at any rate, culminated' she wrote later (L 476–7). No doubt her pleasure was heightened in her memory by contrast with the scene that awaited her on her return home. The Life of Charlotte Brontë had caused a furore far surpassing the criticisms of Mary Barton or Ruth, and Gaskell was threatened with libel action over her allegations about Branwell Brontë's affair with a woman whose identity Gaskell clearly hinted, and whom she accused of ruining Branwell's life, and, indirectly, Charlotte's too. The first and second editions of the Life were hurriedly withdrawn, and an ex-purgated third edition appeared, much to Gaskell's dissatisfaction.

Gaskell had trouble with her health during the writing of the Life, falling ill from exhaustion in September 1856 after a summer spent writing; and in the year or so following its publication she was ill again. She was also troubled with anxieties about Meta, firstly because her engagement to a Captain Hill meant that she would have to follow him to India, then because Meta, hearing something from her fiancé's sisters that destroyed her belief in his character, broke off the engagement. Gaskell took her daughter on a continental trip to restore her spirits, paying for the holiday with the proceeds of 'My Lady Ludlow' (her only substantial work in 1858) and by selling the copyright of some of her earlier published tales.

During the following year she returned to writing with a new enthusiasm, embarking on *Sylvia's Lovers*, for which she was promised £1000. She researched this historical novel thoroughly, visiting Whitby (Monkhaven in the novel) to observe the details of her setting, and taking Meta (an artist of some talent) with her to sketch the views. However, this novel was to take longer than she intended as her work was interrupted over the next few years in various ways: sometimes by family worries like Marianne's intention of converting to Catholicism (she was dissuaded); sometimes by public concerns such as the plight of Manchester cotton workers, out of work due to the American Civil War (Gaskell and her daughters spent the autumn and winter of 1862 engaged in relief work). *Sylvia's Lovers* finally appeared in 1863.

Gaskell, now in her fifties, was declining in health, but she carried on writing and some of her best work dates from this period. 'Cousin Phillis' appeared in the *Cornhill* in monthly instalments over late 1863 and early 1864, and by May 1864 she was planning *Wives and Daughters*, also to be published monthly in the *Cornhill*, an arrangement that suited her much better than the weekly instalments Dickens had wanted for *Household Words*. She spent part of the summer in Switzerland, again finding travel away from home conducive to her writing. By September, though, she was back at home, ill again from overwork. The pattern was repeated the following year: in the spring she visited Paris and continued work on her book, but had to return home when her health deteriorated.

She had wanted for some time to buy a country house well away from Manchester, where her unmarried daughters could live and where she hoped to persuade her husband to retire. Her writing eventually brought her the financial independence to realise this ambition, and in 1865 she bought 'The Lawn' in Alton, Hampshire. She made this purchase without her husband's knowledge; she said it was to surprise him, but she was probably aware that he would be reluctant to move from his Manchester work. In the event neither of them was to live there. In November 1865 she was staying at 'The Lawn' with her daughters when she died suddenly, in the middle of a conversation, of a heart attack. There was one instalment of *Wives and Daughters* still unwritten.

Years of hard work and the emotional strain of publishing had taken their toll of Gaskell. It had taken dextrous juggling to be wife, mother, household manager, part of a lively social circle, and writer; her success was hard-won. Her legacy was a large, varied and impressive *oeuvre* produced over about twenty years, during which her narrative powers had developed from the occasionally gauche and melodramatic *Mary Barton* to the assurance and subtlety of *Wives and Daughters*. The increasing skill and confidence evident in her mature writing suggest that she had found a way of resolving the dilemma of combining the roles of woman and artist.

By the time she wrote *The Life of Charlotte Brontë* Gaskell was expressing a much more serene view of the woman writer's position than appears in the 1850 letters to Eliza Fox. Brontë is seen as split, but in a relatively simple way: her 'existence becomes divided into two parallel currents – her life as Currer Bell, the author; her life as Charlotte Brontë, the woman. There were separate duties belonging to each character – not opposing each other; not impossible, but difficult to be reconciled' (*LCB* 334). The argument of the biography is that Brontë succeeded in this difficult reconciliation, and was as good a woman as she was a great writer. Obviously, Gaskell's polemical purpose here is one determinant of this optimistic reassessment of a problem that, in a private letter to a woman friend and fellow-artist, had appeared more tangled and troubling. Equally important, though, Gaskell's experience during the 1850s had encouraged this greater optimism. Knowing, loving and commemorating her great contemporary was one factor; Gaskell's own success and growing fame was another.

This is not merely a matter of Gaskell's personal history. The degree of public esteem she gained was thanks to aspects of nineteenth-century social change that allowed a woman to speak as a representative of the dominant culture. In sharp contrast to the doubts about a woman's right to write voiced in 1850, a story of 1858, 'My Lady Ludlow', looks back on such doubts as part of a past so safely over as to allow for nostalgia. At one point in the story, Lady Ludlow is surprised to learn that her friend Miss Galindo once contemplated becoming an 'authoress'. On reflection she is glad this came to nothing, for she hates to see 'women usurping men's employments'.[8] This is merely one of her quaint aristocratic prejudices, on a par with her horror of Dissenters and her belief that teaching the poor to read and write will lead to revolution – prejudices that the reader is meant to greet with a smile, because their sting has gone. Lady Ludlow is old-fashioned for her own time, and she dies in 1814, her despotic grip on her community already gently loosened by progressive newcomers. Besides, her kind heart has always softened the effect of her harsh ideas. Elizabeth Gaskell, Unitarian, indefatigable teacher of poor children in Cross Street Chapel and highly respected Victorian author, could afford to be thus tolerant in her depiction of the kind of woman who persecuted her ancestors. For her, becoming a writer did not mean taking over men's employments, but taking up a truly womanly one, in which her feminine sympathies could be turned to good account.

Gaskell's authorial self-confidence resulted from a professional success that made her an exception in a society where most middle-class women had no access to paid employment, and lived domestic lives often extremely constricted by codes of gentility and propriety. Yet if the 'female novelist' seemed an anomaly to many, she was becoming increasingly valued in Gaskell's day. She could be legitimised as representative of a type of feminine authority that played a crucial role within Victorian ideology. The prevailing notion of sexually pure, nurturing, self-sacrificing femininity was based on the separation of the male public sphere from the woman's sphere of privacy and domesticity. In the expanding capitalist economy, man, 'in his rough work in open world, must encounter all peril and trial', but in return for supporting and protecting a dependent wife he expected an emotional refuge in the home created by her feminine goodness: a 'shelter, not only from all injury, but from all terror, doubt and division'.[9] It followed that women need not aspire to the direct economic and political power afforded by 'men's employments', but should be content instead with power in the diffuse form of woman's influence, which supposedly worked indirectly to modify the behaviour of the men in her family. One startling contradiction in this ideology was that the domestic woman was held responsible, through her influence, for public events. Ironically, it was because women were regarded as morally superior that the world's evils could be blamed on them: war, for example, was said to happen because women failed in their sacred duty to prevent it. 'There is not a war in the world, no, nor an injustice, but you women are answerable for it', claimed Ruskin,

> Men, by their nature, are prone to fight . . . It is for you to choose their cause for them, and to forbid them when there is no cause. There is no suffering, no injustice, no misery, in the earth, but the guilt of it lies with you. Men can bear the sight of it, but you should not be able to bear it.[10]

Many Victorian women were ready to accept the burden of a superior womanly nature, but they also realised that domestic influence did not suffice for the task they were given. Women could hardly transmit feminine values into the male world while remaining completely separate from it, and various philanthropic activities that were coded as part of women's sphere, (and are now professionalised as teaching, nursing and social work) were beginning to form a basis for their entry into public life.[11] The woman novelist shared in a gradual Victorian expansion of the women's sphere, a participation eased by her profession's peculiar position within culture. The novel marked an intersection between public and private realms: published, paid for and publicly discussed, but aimed at readers in the home and promoting, through an appeal to feeling, the ideals of domesticity. Its ambiguous position afforded an opportunity for women to exercise the public power usually reserved for men in a form acceptably close to feminine influence. By Gaskell's day the woman novelist was an acceptable, even an admirable figure, partaking of what Nancy Armstrong has called a 'female authority', based on woman's perceived greater understanding of the emotions.[12]

This female authority was, however, granted only on

certain special conditions, which in some respects amounted to a tendency to undermine its existence. Both the granting of this authority and the restrictiveness of its conditions are exemplified in a review of *Ruth* that appeared in the *North British Review* in 1853. It was a particularly significant one for Gaskell, because it was a resoundingly favourable account of the book whose reception in some quarters had reduced the author to fits of crying all one Saturday night, and made her feel like St Stephen stuck with arrows (*L* 220–1). The anonymous writer (Gaskell later established that he was the Christian socialist J. M. Ludlow) claimed to dislike women writers in general, characterising them as 'certain creatures of the female sex, with ink half-way up their fingers, and dirty shawls, and frowsy hair'; nevertheless, he believed that 'the very *best* novels' of the time were women's, because women and novels were alike repositories of feeling:

> if we consider the novel to be the picture of human life . . . as addressed to human feeling, rather than to human taste, judgment, or reason, there seems nothing paradoxical in the view, that women are called to the mastery of this peculiar field of literature. We know, all of us, that if man is the head of humanity, woman is its heart; . . . why should we be surprised to find that her words come more home to us than those of men, where feeling is chiefly concerned?

Unmarried women, in his opinion, could hardly share in this advantage: at best they knew little of (sexual) love, 'the staple of all novel-writing', at worst they might have bitter experience of it; their work, then, stood in danger 'of being abstract, or morbid, or something like – we must mention the word –

immodest'. Good wives and mothers, though, who
refrained from writing until their children were grown,
had far more to offer: 'the moral responsibilities of their
now *completed* lives' [my italics] would lead them to
write so well that, in the reviewer's opinion, the
'supremacy of woman over the novel . . . will go on
widening and deepening . . . only through her shall we
learn what resources there are in it for doing God's
work upon earth'.[13] This was a review holding scant
comfort for Gaskell's unmarried friend Charlotte
Brontë, but for Gaskell herself it was a vindication. 'It is
so truly religious, it makes me swear with delight', she
exclaimed (*L* 222).

It is interesting that this tribute to Gaskell as
maternal and religious teacher should be called up by
Ruth, the very novel that to some readers epitomised
the dangers of immoral fiction. Members of her
husband's congregation had burned the first volume of
this story of an unmarried mother. The reviewer's
insistence on Gaskell's womanliness, and the slur on
the modesty of other women writers, must be read as
defensive tactics, but at the same time the review
outlines a vision of the ideal woman writer that had a
widespread appeal in the nineteenth century. Gaskell
appears here as an example of the ideal: the good
mother who writes; consequently her controversial
treatment of sexual issues can be praised as the
expression of an essentially maternal concern for the
weaker members of society, rather than disturbing the
reviewer with the personal bitterness, even rebelliousness, associated with Charlotte Brontë's works. Brontë's
novels 'have in them a something harsh, rough,
unsatisfying, some say all but unwomanly, as compared to the full, and wholesome, and most womanly
perfection of [Gaskell]'.[14]

Gaskell was not a woman to accept without demur a

praise so dependent on the disparagement of other women, and she took Ludlow to task over his treatment of Brontë (see below, chapter 3). Nevertheless she was delighted by Ludlow's description of a maternal authority so close to the one she advocates in *Ruth* and was developing for herself. Ruth's sin is a result of her being deprived of a mother's care, and her own motherhood, for all society labels it illegitimate, becomes the working of her salvation. Ludlow acknowledges the point and attributes Gaskell's rendering of it to her own motherhood: 'the authoress of Ruth is a mother, and the duties of hallowed motherhood have taught her own pure soul what its blessings may be to the fallen'.[15] As a mother, Gaskell has the right to write even shocking works: she has the authority to teach and change her society.

Yet Ludlow's concept of maternal authority is problematic, not only because it is divisive, excluding childless women and mothers themselves until their children are grown (Gaskell herself, whose first novel was written while Julia was a baby, does not quite fit the picture of the ideal mother writer), but because he loses faith in it at precisely the point when it becomes a challenge to the authority of the father. He agrees with the author of *Ruth* on practically every point but one, namely Ruth's crucial rejection of the father of her child when he offers marriage. She rejects him because as a mother she fears the influence a bad father will have on his son, and the rejection expresses Gaskell's repudiation of the patriarchal assumption that haunts Ruth in nightmares: the idea that the child 'belonged of legal right to the father' (R 290). Ludlow's review asks the author

Is she quite sure that Ruth has the right, when Mr Donne offers to marry her, and give their son all the advantages of his position, to reject his offer? . . . Has she such complete dominion over Leonard that she dares, of her own choice, deprive him of his father?[16]

The problems besetting maternal authority may be better understood by turning to Margaret Homans's account of women's writing in the nineteenth century. Homans uses theories of language acquisition derived from the psychoanalyst Jacques Lacan to suggest that nineteenth-century women writers were deeply affected by a cultural myth that language is properly gendered male. Her use of the word 'myth' is significant: she sees the psychoanalytic account of language acquisition not as revealing a truth but as a particular expression of a long-standing belief, within patriarchal culture, in the masculinity of language and culture. This myth, she argues, has existed in varying forms in different eras, and so can have a real effect on women's writing. Lacan need not be right about the way language is acquired for his work to describe a set of assumptions that affected writers like Gaskell.

Lacanian theory sees the acquisition of language as predicated on psychic separation from the mother and therefore symbolically entailing her absence. It posits for all children an initial bond with the mother, in which an illusory sense of wholeness is experienced, followed by the intervention of the father, whose presence interrupts the bond and institutes a separation between child and mother. The young boy becomes aware of sexual difference, and of his own difference from his mother, at the same time as he begins to acquire language. Language, like the process of acquiring psychic identity, works through differentiation and separation, a sign having meaning through its difference from other signs. Learning language, the precondition for taking an active part in culture (in

Lacanian terms, the symbolic order), is psychically linked with differentiation from the mother. The boy has lost the initial wholeness with the mother but acquired language, and the promise of mastery within culture, instead. Loss of the mother is thus felt as necessary, even as substitutes for her are sought. In Homans's version of the theory, language creates a series of figures that can be substituted for the mother's body. The mother is identified with the literal, the lost real body, and language with the figural, a series of signs that substitute for the literal. Paradoxically Homans can also posit the existence of a 'literal language' that recalls the early, non-verbal communication between mother and infant.

In Lacanian theory, the girl's relation to the acquisition of language is different. Although her initial bond with the mother is also interrupted, she does not acquire her identity through differentiation from her mother. In Homans's words, 'the daughter discovers that she is the same as her mother and different from her father, so her relationship to her mother contradicts, rather than reinforces (as in the case of the son), the dependence of the symbolic order on the absence of the mother'.[17] In Lacanian theory this difference is a disadvantage because the female has less incentive to turn from the mother and enter the symbolic order. Her mastery of language will be incomplete, and she will not be among the builders of culture. The theory has obvious negative implications for women's ability to be writers. Feminist psychoanalysts, however, look at the girl's situation differently. Homans develops her revision of Lacan by using the work of Nancy Chodorow, who argues that women do not separate from the mother and what she represents so completely as men do, and in becoming mothers themselves they attempt to reproduce the pleasures of the early mother–child bond. Homans uses this idea to argue that the daughter enters the realm of language and culture but without giving up the bond with the mother. 'The daughter . . . speaks two languages at once. Along with symbolic language, she retains the literal or presymbolic language that the son represses.'[18] The woman writer, then, may write differently from men, her work embodying the connection with the mother, but to the extent that she does so, her work will be devalued.

Homans applies this idea to women writers in the nineteenth century, who wrote in the shadow of the Romantic movement. She argues that they may have felt a special identification with nature, which in Romantic thought is maternal, and is, in the work of male Romantic poets, that which is lost and which poetry attempts to re-create. If the woman writer identifies herself, or is identified with, mother nature, it is more difficult for her to legitimate her work within culture through the use of the 'masculine' figurative language, which is associated with separation from the mother. She is faced with a dilemma: how to take up the maternal position recommended by her society, and to write within a post-Romantic tradition that tends to define the writer's position in terms of 'his' separation from nature and the maternal? Analysing Gaskell's confrontation with this problem, Homans concludes that Gaskell discoversed that 'to be at once a mother and a writer is to be divided in two'.[19]

This account of the access of nineteenth-century women to cultural authority differs markedly from that offered by Nancy Armstrong, who sees the nineteenth-century novel as a feminised discourse offering a specifically female authority, so that the Victorian novelist (even when male) can to be said to write as a woman. Critical of that feminist writing that sees women only in terms of gender, ignoring class and race, and which tends to type women as victims and to see any manifestation of female subjectivity as a form of resistance, Armstrong emphasises that middle-class women in the nineteenth century had real power within their culture. Indeed, they are important creators of middle-class power in the first place:

> those cultural functions which we automatically attribute to and embody as women . . . mother, nurse, teacher, social worker . . . have been just as instrumental in bringing the new middle classes into power and maintaining their dominance as all the economic take-offs and political breakthroughs we automatically attribute to men.[20]

One of the important cultural functions of the Victorian woman was that of novelist. The female authority Armstrong ascribes to the Victorian woman novelist was granted and used by the middle class in a bid to naturalise its own political power. Victorian novels, presenting love and marriage as central issues, allowed political resistance to be displaced onto a sexual conflict, which was then resolved through romantic love. Thus class conflict was made to appear ultimately unimportant. One example of what Armstrong means might be in *North and South*, where, it could be argued, the struggle between capitalist and workers is ultimately seen as less important than the sexual struggle between Margaret Hale and John Thornton, a struggle that is resolved on the last page in an affirmation of romantic love and marriage. Armstrong argues that to read such stories of sexual love as involving only sexuality, ignoring their effectiveness as political containment, is to participate in their displacement of political resistance.

Armstrong's work is extremely valuable in its ability to account for the wide political range of women's writing and for the great public success of women novelists in the Victorian era. However, representing power for women as always co-opted by class interests, she ignores any use of female power for resistance. In her account, Elizabeth Gaskell appears simply as an agent of the counter-revolutionary middle class: she and Charles Dickens are put together as writers in whose hands 'domestic fiction carries the process of suppressing political resistance into the domain of popular literature'.[21] In contrast, Homans presents Gaskell as a woman writer who, though forced like others to use the language authorised by her culture, was bolder than many 'in her claims for writing as a woman', and thus to some extent able to challenge male-dominated structures of authority. Far from being a middle-class spokeswoman, she is less canonical than George Eliot or Emily Brontë because of her radical claim 'that there may be other ways for women to write' beyond the alternatives of being masculine or subordinate.[22]

I have given some space to articulating a difference between two writers who deal with the relation of women to language and culture in Gaskell's time, because I think that this debate concerning the extent and political tendency of women's cultural authority is central to Gaskell criticism today. To simplify, it is a debate between two feminist positions, one informed by Marxism, the other by psychoanalysis. Armstrong's and Homans's opposition turns on the gendering of language. While both would agree that the gendering of language is a cultural construct and not a reflection of a natural state, their accounts of nineteenth-century culture, concentrating, respectively, on a cultural myth that language is male, and a cultural granting of female authority, seem mutually contradictory. I do not want to offer an easy reconciliation between these warring members; but it is possible to see both accounts as containing some truth, and both as relevant to Gaskell, because the contradiction between them is a contradiction displayed by nineteenth-century culture itself. The female authority described by Armstrong is, as she shows, based on emotion, and thus would be perceived as (however much to be revered) ultimately subordinate to a reason perceived as masculine. This can be seen, for example, in the well-worn head–heart distinction made in Ludlow's review of *Ruth*, quoted earlier: 'if man is the head of humanity, woman is its heart'. Female authority applies in the novel rather than in the supposedly higher form, poetry. Thus Victorians could both venerate female, and particularly maternal, authority as constituted in language (the language of novels) and, simultaneously, reserve an ultimately higher, more intellectual, authority for other discourses (poetry as opposed to prose, or science as opposed to fiction), which could then be imagined as masculine (and would take the position given to 'language' and 'the symbolic order' in Homans's revised Lacanian scheme).

As a novelist, Gaskell was presented with a kind of authority by her culture, but a compromised and subordinate one. She was part of middle-class culture, but neither securely entrenched in nor entirely colluding with it. Her gender and class positions pulled against each other: as a woman she wanted and needed to challenge existing structures; as a middle-class woman she had a good deal of power at stake in them. Her religion, like her gender, placed her in an ambiguous position relative to cultural authority. As a Unitarian she was a member of a group that remembered past persecutions, and felt an obligation to speak out a truth that was in conflict with the doctrines of the established church, and through this, the hierarchy of authority in nineteenth-century England. Yet Unitarians in her time, especially in her own Manchester, were in positions of financial, social and political power, which they could use to help the oppressed – or to oppress them further.

I think that both the 'counter-revolutionary' and the 'radical' Gaskell are critical creations that echo some aspect of a complex figure. Gaskell's writing frequently expresses a tension between a reasoned commitment to a radical position outside the dominant culture, and a temperamental, and aesthetic, preference for moving inside it. She felt this tension as a woman, combining admiration for the feminist Barbara Bodichon with a distaste for her rebellious attitudes:

> She is . . . a strong fighter against the established opinions of the world, – which always goes against my – what shall I call it? – *taste* – (that is not the word,) but I can't help admiring her noble bravery, and respecting – while I don't personally *like* her.
>
> (*L* 607)

She felt it as a Unitarian, unable to agree with the Church's doctrines but tempted by her love of poetry and music to attend its services.

Gaskell, then, woman and Unitarian, was a member of two groups who in nineteenth-century England were gaining a new degree of authority and becoming able to speak as representatives of, not only in opposition to, the dominant culture. At the same time neither group was unequivocally accepted at the centre of power. Each group was gaining some power and might therefore take a favourable view of recent social change, but they might also be conscious of the dangers of becoming identified with the culture they entered instead of changing it. Tension is created between the desire to be at the centre of culture, authorised by it, and the desire to remain on the margins.

Of the multiplicity of Elizabeth Gaskells I am concentrating on the interplay between two of them: the authorised spokeswoman for Victorian society – confident, tolerant and advocating progress, reconciliation and the healing of divisions; and the hesitant, self-divided writer conscious of a radical religious heritage, and speaking, as Unitarian and as woman, on the margins of her society, with the outsider's eye described by Virginia Woolf: 'alien and critical'.[23]

2 Giving Utterance:
Mary Barton

The gradual development of the Unitarians from a persecuted group, strongly associated with radical politics, to a socially powerful one, many of whose members were rich capitalists in growing industrial centres like Manchester, opened up gaps between theory and practice; and it is these gaps to which Gaskell's first novel calls attention.[1] It has been shown that her descriptions of working-class conditions and attitudes depend a great deal (to the extent of verbatim quotation of a number of paragraphs) on the Unitarian publications, *The Reports of the Ministry to the Poor*, for the years covered in her novel (1839–42).[2] These reports were themselves fuelled by the desire to confront rich Unitarians not only with the poverty but with the feelings of their employees. Gaskell shared that desire, and wrote to recall the prosperous to a sense of Christian charity. Her targets were her own friends, members of her husband's congregation, the leading figures in Manchester society; and while readers like Carlyle and Dickens were deeply impressed by her novel, the reaction closer to home was much less favourable. The *Edinburgh Review* article on *Mary Barton*, for example, which criticised Gaskell for dwelling on the workers' difficulties and ignoring the sufferings of unsuccessful manufacturers, was written by William Greg, a manufacturer, Unitarian and friend.[3]

The novel, then, was not only, as Monica Fryckstedt calls it, 'a challenge to Christian England', but more specifically, and painfully, a challenge to Unitarian

Manchester. It was a challenge Gaskell felt authorised to make because it included a challenge to herself. As part of the prosperous middle-class Unitarian group she was conscious of the gap between her own experience and that of the poor and oppressed who were championed by the Gospels: but it was a gap that she hoped in some way to bridge through her writing.

'Ay, ma'am, but have ye ever seen a child clemmed to death?', a Manchester man is supposed to have challenged Gaskell, when she was trying to talk him out of his hatred of the rich.[4] She hadn't: but she saw her son die of scarlet fever, and wrote her first novel in the midst of her grief. Her tragic hero John Barton is embittered by an agony based on her own, but made still more excruciating because it could easily have been avoided if he had had money. Before the start of the novel's main action, Barton's son Tom had caught scarlet fever. Unlike Willie Gaskell he showed signs of recovery, but he died because his father could not afford the food needed to build up his strength; while the employer who had laid Barton off because of business failure could still buy luxuries. John Barton's hatred of the employing class dates from this, and when more quiescent friends try to argue that the masters too suffer in bad times, Gaskell makes him echo the words that had haunted her: 'Han they ever seen a child o' their'n die for want o' food?' (*MB* 105).

It is typical of Gaskell that she turns this potent expression of the difference between rich and poor into the starting-point for an exploration of their common humanity. Without shying from the truth that poverty was the cause of the high infant mortality in Manchester, she took love for children and grief at their loss as the feeling connecting people of all classes. In *Mary Barton* parental love and grief are repeatedly stressed. John Barton has lost his son; the Wilsons' twin boys, seen with their proud parents in the opening scene in Green Heys Field, die of typhoid fever in the course of the narrative; Mary Barton's aunt Esther explains how she took to prostitution in a vain attempt to save her little daughter's life; Job Legh tells of the shock of his daughter's death and his journey home from London with his baby granddaughter, when he was helped by a bereaved mother for 'poor little Johnnie's sake' (MB 153). When Barton, as the instrument of union revenge on the employers, assassinates Harry Carson, the act is mainly significant as the killing of a son. It makes Carson suffer in the way so many of his workers have suffered, in the way this novel presents as the epitome of human suffering, by losing a child. Revenge is his first thought, but he is eventually brought to forgive the murderer; and the final outcome is that he resolves to work for better industrial relations. Recent improvements in employment practices in Manchester are attributed to his 'stern, thoughtful mind, which submitted to be taught by suffering' (460).

Mary Barton has been labelled an 'industrial novel', and it certainly contains many of the right ingredients for one: it is set in the Manchester of the hungry forties, and John Barton takes part in the Chartist demonstration of 1839; it deals with the relation between employers and employed, mentions the hours and conditions of work, and includes the narrative of a strike and its attendant negotiations and violence. Yet Barton the weaver is never seen at his trade, and Jem Wilson only once at his foundry, when he is about to leave it; while Mary Barton's apprenticeship at the dressmaker's is more important as the background to Harry Carson's courtship than in its own right. It is family life in industrial society that interests Gaskell. The Bartons' house and Alice Wilson's cellar, described in loving detail, are 'Dutch interiors' worthy of George

Eliot; and they are the settings for the family relationships and neighbourly friendships that animate the
novel.

Children are the focus of emotion in the novel, and
are often given a symbolic significance. Carson is
converted to forgiveness after a chance encounter in the
street with a little girl who pleads on behalf of a boy
who has knocked her over: '*He did not know what he was
doing*, did you, little boy?' (438). Her words echo
Barton's cry of remorse, and both echo the words of
Christ's forgiveness on the cross. If this fluttering little
'fairy-child' (437) seems the product of a very heavy-
handed Victorian sentimentalism, in the context of the
novel as a whole her influence over Carson does not
seem so improbable. The reader has been prepared by
other, more successful uses of chance-met children.
John Barton pauses on his way to murder one man's
son, in order to help another child find its way home;
and as he listens patiently to glean meaning from the
little boy's imperfect speech, he demonstrates the
novel's cardinal virtue. In this episode too there are
biblical overtones: Barton is acting like the Good
Shepherd who searches for the stray, at the very time
he is in danger of becoming a lost sheep himself. On
another occasion, Mary returns home in agony, believing that her lover Jem has murdered Harry Carson, and
she meets a little Italian boy begging for food. His
bodily hunger becomes a sign of his innocence: Mary
cries with the agony of experience: 'Oh, lad, hunger is
nothing – nothing!' (284) In each of these encounters
the adult sufferer is like, as well as unlike, the child.
Carson, himself a man of working-class origins who
has pushed his way up in the world, is more obviously
like the rough errand boy who 'brushed rudely past,
not much caring whom he hurt, so that he got along'
(437), but he learns to forgive like the injured girl.

Mary, like the Italian boy with his cry of 'mamma mia', is in desperate need of a mother's guidance, which comes to her that night when her aunt Esther returns, looking exactly like Mary's dead mother. John Barton's encounter suggests that even a murderer is only a straying child. Children, the centre of Gaskell's social vision, also indicate the religious dimension that for her transcends the social: all her characters, in the last analysis, are children of God.

Whatever else it means, then, Gaskell's emphasis on children and family responsibilities should not be taken as evidence of a narrowness of view, a 'feminine' inability to deal with the 'real' issues of industrialism. It is true that she often expresses self-doubt when her narrative enters the 'masculine' spheres of industrial relations or murder investigation. Explaining the events leading up to the strike, the narrator is unsure if she can command the technical terms used by masters and men; and when Mary searches her father's pockets after the murder the narrator does not know whether to call what she finds bullets or shot (300). But these hesitations have the main effect of encouraging the reader to trust so homely and unpretentious a narrator; and when, in the preface, Gaskell denies all knowledge of 'Political Economy, or the theories of trade' (38), the self-deprecation is ironic. The theories of political economy formulated by liberal thinkers were readily available, and several reviewers of Gaskell's novel obligingly pointed them out to her. It was useless to interfere between masters and men with any employment legislation: wages would find their own level. Workers should save enough during periods of employment to help themselves when they were out of work, and those who did not were poor through their own improvidence. The system was not unfair: the owners of capital, because they were risking their property in business ventures, were entitled to all the profits from them.[5] By claiming to know nothing of all this Gaskell was really directing the reader's view to what she thought more important concerns.

Carlyle (as her novel's motto first indicates) was her mentor. He attacked political economy in influential works like *Chartism* and *Past and Present*, arguing against the philosophy of *laissez-faire*, against the belief that cash payment for work done was the sole obligation of employers to their workers, and against the very idea that workers' conditions could be understood by reference to wage levels: 'how many "demands" are there, entirely indispensable, which have to go elsewhere than to the shops, and pro- duce quite other than cash, before they can get their supply!'[6] Writing about workers' demands in *Mary Barton*, Gaskell, too, emphasised the need for much more than economic improvement, advocating a transformation in the human relationship between employers and employed. Before this could happen, the middle-class public must be jolted into under- standing what was happening to the working class. Gaskell, aiming to do just that in her novel, was answering the call Carlyle had made when he attacked public ignorance of the 'Condition of England', and claimed that this could not be dispelled by statistics or theory, but only by attending to the human facts.

Marx, of course, was to offer an analysis of the relation between labour and capital very different from that offered by 'political economy'; but the labour theory of value was not available to Gaskell, and she would not have used it anyway. Marx's analysis rests on the fundamental assumption of the different interests of different classes: Gaskell, approaching the subject from the point of view of religious principle rather than economic analysis, was deeply convinced that everyone in society shared the same interests, and thought it *'wicked . . .* to excite class against class' (*L* 67). This meant that she was unable to fight the political economists on their own ground: sharing their assumption that employers and employed must rise and fall together, she could not counter the common argument, put forward by the employers in *Mary Barton*, that workers should accept lower wage levels when their masters are having trade problems. Her criticism is not of the employers' decision but their refusal to communicate it properly. However, while her direct statements often pander to the dominant economic arguments of her class, she offers in the fabric of her story an implicit, but devastating attack on them. Like Carlyle, she makes the political economists' mode of thought her target. Rather than prove them wrong in their own terms, she brings in a different, religious, frame of reference, in which their work becomes irrelevant.

Take the argument that the workers are reduced to poverty by their own improvidence, easily 'proved' by the examples of one or two who had worked their way up by exceptional diligence and luck. Direct comment on the idea in *Mary Barton* takes the form of nervous corroboration. The workman thinks that only the workers suffer in bad times, but the narrator insists:

> I know that this is not really the case; and I know what is the truth in such matters: but what I wish to impress is what the workman feels and thinks. True, that with child-like improvidence, good times will often dissipate his grumbling, and make him forget all prudence and foresight. (60)

However, the whole force of the narrative pushes against such comments. Gaskell encourages her reader to enter into the simple pleasures, a necessary part of social existence, which are enough to prevent people so poor from saving. The process begins with the opening scene in Green Heys Field where the workers are taking a probably unofficial day off to enjoy the May sunshine and the countryside instead of laying up money for future contingencies, and continues when the Bartons give a tea-party for the Wilsons afterwards, carefully reckoning the cost of fried ham and eggs for seven people. Mrs Barton tells Mary to buy a pound of ham; on her husband's 'say two pounds, missis, and don't be stingy' (50), she compromises at a pound and a half. Their friends tactfully pretend not to hear the discussion and plan to repay the hospitality in the future; and the tea is considered a rare treat. Gaskell makes it difficult for the most churlish of readers to disapprove of her characters' enjoyments, and she makes them poignantly short-lived. The next day, Mrs Barton is dead and her grieving husband has the additional problem of being left short of money by what Gaskell, with quiet irony, terms the evening's 'extravagance' (58).

Other examples of the workers' 'improvidence' abound: short of funds, Barton pawns some clothes for five shillings, not to support himself but to buy provisions for the even poorer Davenport family. When Margaret Jennings makes some money by singing ballads for a music lecturer on a Lancashire tour, she gives much of it away: a sovereign to Mary Barton, some to Mrs Davenport as payment for nursing Alice Wilson. Jem Wilson does carefully invest the two or three hundred pounds he makes from his invention, but not on his own behalf: he buys annuities for his mother and aunt. Friendship, family love, mutual help and hospitality make up these characters' main pleasures in life, and Gaskell shows that for these people to save for themselves, as the political economists advise, would be unthinkably selfish.[7]

This is nowhere stated as an argument, but it emerges from the overall picture of Manchester life. Gaskell's aim is to arouse interest in the whole of her characters' lives, and a sympathetic identification with them: not just pity, which can so easily shade into contempt. That is why the few middle-class characters are given so little emphasis: middle-class readers are left with no option but to centre their attention on the working-class characters and to enter into their lives in a way that makes the judgements of political economists seem quite irrelevant.

Gaskell is aiming at an audience of her own class. Turning from the economic to the emotional and religious connections between people of different classes, her whole emphasis is on the necessity for communication. Speaking and listening make up the novel's central theme. Gaskell accuses her own class of not listening to the workers. She aims to give the workers a voice and make the middle class listen. As she explains in her preface, her purpose was to speak for the workers:

> The more I reflected on this unhappy state of things between those so bound to each other by common interests, as the employers and the employed must ever be, the more anxious I became to give some utterance to the agony which, from time to time, convulses this dumb people. (37–8)

One of her methods is her careful reproduction of Manchester dialect, along with explanatory footnotes (provided by her husband) that translate her characters' words and implicitly defend them by showing their roots in Anglo-Saxon, or similar forms in Shake-speare or Ben Jonson. If this, at times, seems rather condescending treatment, it does indicate how seriously Gaskell regards her dialect voices: they are not there (as dialect in novels of the time so often was) for comic effect. The rhythms of John Barton's speeches may be artistically formed to give him his character-istic, cumulative eloquence, but his words are still based on close observation of the vocabulary, pro-nunciation and syntax of the Manchester workers. This is one indication of Gaskell's real respect for her characters, and shows her fleshing out Carlyle's idea of the importance of the working-class voice. It is important, too, that for her it is a multiple voice. Barton's expressions of the workers' grievances are balanced by Job Legh's stories from his past, which illustrate how the workers help each other, and by Margaret's songs. When John Barton sets out for London as part of the Chartist delegation of 1839, it is the occasion for a chorus of friends' voices suggesting various demands to be put to Parliament. The point is neither to endorse all the claims nor to mock the speakers' naïvety, but simply to give them their say.

Gaskell is interested in the workers' culture in the widest sense, and especially in their poetic tradition. Here again she shows her affinities with Carlyle, who had greeted the poetry of Ebenezer Elliott (1781–1849), the 'Corn-Law Rhymer', as

a voice coming from the deep Cyclopean forges, where Labour, in real soot and sweat, beats with his thousand hammers 'the red son of the furnace'; . . . an intelligible voice from the hitherto Mute and Irrational . . . to which voice, in several respects significant enough, let good ear be given.[8]

Like Carlyle's essay on 'Corn-Law Rhymes', *Mary Barton* promotes working-class poetry for a middle-class readership. Elliott himself is quoted: his poems provide mottos for four of Gaskell's chapters (chapters 4, 5, 10 and 34). The weaver Samuel Bamford, best known for his *Passages in the Life of a Radical* (1840–44), receives extensive coverage, his poem 'God help the poor' being read aloud in full by Job Legh and copied by Mary on a piece of paper that later plays an important part in the plot. Anonymous poems are quoted too, like 'The Oldham Weaver', a ballad of hard times written not long after the battle of Waterloo. All these are important, not just as a way of adding colour to the novel, but as means of letting working people's voices be heard.

As Gaskell's own chosen examples show, poetry was one medium for working-class expressions of protest. When Carlyle reviews the Corn-Law Rhymes, he treats Elliott's poetry and his political message as distinct; he praises the poet, but dissociates himself from the politics, though he finds Elliott's rebellious attitude understandable. 'Nevertheless, under all disguises of the Radical, the Poet is still recognisable: a certain music breathes through all dissonances, as the prophecy and ground-tone of returning harmony; the man, as we said, is of a poetical nature'.[9] The picture Carlyle draws of the Corn-Law Rhymer can be related to the composite picture Gaskell gives of the Manchester working class. The workers in *Mary Barton*, like Carlyle's Ebenezer Elliott, are deplorably but understandably rebellious. Under all the 'disguise' of Chartist agitation, she reveals their true 'poetical nature', which is particularly evident in Job Legh and his granddaughter Margaret, a storyteller and a singer, not protesters; but clear, too, in John Barton himself, whose rhetorical talents are put to political use. His 'ready kind of rough Lancashire eloquence, arising out of the fulness of his heart, which was very stirring to men similarly circumstanced, who liked to hear their feelings put into words' (*MB* 220), makes him a class spokesman like the working-class poets Gaskell quotes.

The 'visionary' quality (220) that links John Barton to the poets indicates his deep attachment to his fellow man, and leads to his commitment to the trade union; and with tragic irony, it leads him eventually to murder. The theme of speech and silence, so central to *Mary Barton*, is crucial here. Silence is the great danger in the novel, always the prelude to violence; and throughout the novel Gaskell is warning her middle-class readership that if they will not listen to the workers there will be a dangerous silence. She places the warning, appropriately, in poetic form, when she prints 'The Oldham Weaver'. On the surface this song appears to be introduced as an amusing curiosity, a 'complete Lancashire ditty', chosen by Alice and sung by Margaret, whose smile at the choice suggests she does not take it very seriously. The narrator, too, treats the song rather deprecatingly, admitting that it might seem merely funny when read, but assuring her readers that it has pathos for someone who has seen the distress it describes. If we attend to the words, though, this dialect ditty contains a threat. The speaker is a poor cotton-weaver who complains that he is starving and has no clothes, and describes how the bailiffs take away all his furniture, right down to the last stool 'whopped up' from underneath him and Marget. In the second verse, he answers a friend who advises him to keep quiet:

Owd Dicky o' Billy's kept telling me lung,
Wee s'd ha' better toimes if I'd but howd my tung,

Oi've howden my tung, till oi've near stopped my
breath . . . (72)

The weaver refuses to hold his tongue and be resigned
to his miseries; but the last verse of his song hints at a
silence that will be the opposite of resignation.

Eawr Marget declares had hoo cloo'as to put on,
Hoo'd goo up to Lunnon an' talk to' th' greet mon;
An' if things were na awtered when there hoo had
   been,
Hoo's fully resolved t'sew up meawth an' eend;
   Hoo's neawt to say again t'king,
   But hoo loikes a fair thing,
An' hoo says hoo can tell when hoo's hurt. (73)

Marget's project of going to London to talk to the great
man foreshadows the 1839 Chartist petition to Parliament, which raises such grand hopes in Gaskell's
characters later in the novel. When John Barton returns
from taking part in presenting that petition, things have
not altered, and like Marget he is resolved to sew up
his mouth: 'I'll not speak of it no more' (145). It is
a move towards the breakdown of communication
between classes that eventually results in the murder
of Harry Carson, Gaskell's symbolic equivalent for
revolution.

John Barton claims proudly, 'I'd scorn to speak for
mysel' (105). Like her hero, Gaskell intends in *Mary
Barton* to speak on others' behalf, and she is at her best
where she eschews narrative comment and gives free
rein to her characters' eloquence. But it is, of course,
impossible for her to abdicate completely. For all her
effort to 'give voice' to the workers it is not possible for
her to be the voice of the working class. Just as Carlyle
is selective in the way he listens to Ebenezer Elliott,

trying to shut out the political message in order to hear the harmony, Gaskell is selective about which working-class voices she transmits. This is made clear in chapter 16 of the novel, where the decision to murder Harry Carson is taken. In this chapter we are given a good deal of John Barton's eloquence. His voice is heard, as always, on behalf of others:

> It makes me more than sad, it makes my heart burn within me, to see that folk can make a jest of earnest men; of chaps, who comed to ask for a bit o' fire for th' old granny, as shivers in the cold; for a bit o' bedding, and some warm clothing to the poor wife as lies in labour on th' damp flags; and for victuals for the childer, whose little voices are getting too faint and weak to cry aloud wi' hunger. (238)

Barton's compassionate nature is further demonstrated when he explains why he missed a worker's meeting earlier in the day: he had been, first, to visit a union member imprisoned for throwing vitriol at a strike-breaker, and then to see the blinded victim. It is Barton's tender-heartedness that leads him to murder, for it is this scene that has pushed him into shouting for violence against the masters instead of against fellow workers. Harry Carson's murder is accordingly planned. However, Barton's associates had already been pointed in the direction of violence at the earlier meeting that the hero missed. There, a shadowy union representative, specified only as an outsider, a 'gentleman from London', had been the first to advocate violence, and is clearly in some sense to blame for the decision to kill Harry Carson. His eloquence is said to stir the workers, who are greatly taken with his 'gift of the gab', yet his speech, in contrast to Barton's, is not given us direct. It is left suspended in the silence between one paragraph and the next:

> rising like a great orator, with his right arm outstretched, his left in the breast of his waistcoat, he began to declaim, with a forced theatrical voice.
> After a burst of eloquence . . . (236–7)

There are limits to Gaskell's project of speaking on behalf of others: she makes her working men speak but she gives no voice to the representative of the workers' organisation. In a novel built on the theme of people's need to listen to each other's voices, it is instructive to find Gaskell's own silent spot, the voice she does not want to listen to or convey to us.

Women's voices are of particular interest in the novel. Gaskell's attitude to them is somewhat equivocal. A woman's guiding influence in her family is seen as very important, and when John Barton's wife dies he loses 'one of the ties which bound him down to the gentle humanities of earth' (58) and is left vulnerable to the somewhat sinister influence of the trade union movement, which draws him away from home and family to meetings where no woman's voice is heard, and where ultimately speech gives way to violence. It is one measure of the hardening caused by his wife's death that Barton refuses to listen to Esther's warning about the danger Mary is in from Harry Carson: blaming her disappearance for the shock that caused his wife's death, he will have nothing to do with her. Yet if he had listened, Esther's speech would only have given him an additional motive for hating Harry Carson; and when she does succeed in telling her tale, to Jem, all that is achieved is the quarrel with Harry that leads to Jem being suspected after the murder. Esther's voice only becomes helpful when she finally manages to communicate with Mary, whom she avoids at first out of shame. When Esther brings her niece the gun-wadding she found at the scene of the crime, she enables Mary to work out the truth about the murder, to destroy the evidence, and eventually to prove Jem's innocence without revealing her father's guilt. This public action becomes Mary's one occasion for speaking out. Because she will not implicate her father, her evidence in court cannot clear Jem (she achieves that by finding Will Wilson to testify to Jem's alibi), but she uses the occasion to make a public declaration of the love she had earlier denied to him. By telling the truth about her love she offers a kind of unconscious compensation for concealing the truth that might save him. In Esther's and Mary's crucial revelations, taboos governing women's speech are broken: the prostitute communicates with the 'unfallen' woman, and a woman makes a public statement of her love. Gaskell seems to be implying that it is by breaking out of the constraints on their speech that women can do good by their communications. Again, it is emphasised that neither speaks on her own behalf. Esther speaks to help Mary, and Mary's public speech, like the whole of her efforts in connection with the trial, are to help another.

Yet even this breaking of womanly silence is hedged with qualifications. Esther's shame remains, and she can neither tell Mary the truth about her life nor receive her kiss. Mary's declaration of love is only justified by the extremity of the circumstances; and it is worth noting that these circumstances would never have arisen if she had found a way of letting Jem know of her love when she first realised it. Gaskell explicitly endorses the maidenly modesty that makes it impossible for her even to drop him a hint, and Margaret Jennings, the epitome of selfless womanly nobility, is

made to add her advice to Mary's instinct. In the rest of
the novel, speaking and listening are cardinal virtues,
but when it comes to a woman speaking of love, the
standards of maidenly heroism must prevail. After
the trial Mary goes mad from the double strain of what
she has concealed and what she has revealed, and she
loses for a while all power of speech. When she
recovers, her public effort is over and she looks
forward to a quieter existence as Jem's wife.[10] In the
normal life she returns to, the ethic of quiet resignation
put forward by good women like Margaret Jennings
and Alice Wilson will be restored.

Gaskell, then, has some reservations about the
speaking out that she advocates, depicts and enacts in
the writing of *Mary Barton*. They were reservations
shared by Carlyle, one of her most appreciative
readers, who wrote her a letter of congratulation that at
one point she considered her only 'real true gain' from
the novel (*L* 68). He began by welcoming hers as a
woman's voice, addressing the anonymous author:
'Dear Madam (for I catch the treble in that fine
melodious voice very well)', and went on to praise her
for giving voice to 'a huge subject, which has lain
dumb too long, and really ought to speak for itself, and
tell us its meaning a little, if there be any voice in it at
all'.[11] Yet at the end of his letter, after expressing the
hope that she will write more books, he added: 'and to
do *silently* good actions, which I believe is very much
more indispensable!'[12] Gaskell agreed, and particularly
cherished this part of his letter (*L* 70). Indeed there is a
sense in which she might have considered the writing
of *Mary Barton* itself as a kind of 'silently good action'.
She is (almost) silent about her personal concerns: the
melodious voice speaks for others.

In *Mary Barton* Gaskell gives utterance to the voices
of working men and women, normally not heard by

the middle-class public – voices silenced by the re-
strictions of class and in the women's case those of
gender too. The problems inherent in speaking on
behalf of others dog her narrative, leading to occasional
condescension, awkward fluctuations of narrative
voice, and sometimes a distorting takeover of the voice
of working-class protest. A crucial instance occurs
when the dying Barton explains himself: 'I was tore in
two often-times, between my sorrow for poor suffering
folk, and my trying to love them as caused their
sufferings (to my mind)' (441). In his qualifying aside
we hear not his voice but Gaskell's, anxiously con-
ciliatory towards her own class. To speak for others, in
this example, becomes to silence them. The Victorian
working class, without a voice in Parliament and with
limited access to the various forms of publication,
could be seen by the middle class as 'this dumb
people', as the novel's preface puts it. While Gaskell's
novel is committed to proving this definition untrue,
by representing the people's voices in multiple ways,
the representation involves distortion, not only when a
middle-class voice obviously intervenes, but in the
narrative's interpretation of the workers' speech and in
its selective silences. As a realist committed to the belief
that her art could reveal the truth about the social
world, Gaskell could see her representation of the
Manchester people's language as a benevolent and
truthful act of communication between classes. In the
age of postmodernism, with its distrust of the claims of
representation, her endeavour may well appear in a
less favourable light. We might apply to *Mary Barton*
the strictures that have been applied to certain kinds of
documentary photography:

'concerned' or . . . 'victim' photography overlooks
the constitutive role of its own activity, which is held

to be merely representative (the 'myth' of photo-graphic transparency and objectivity). Despite his or her benevolence in representing those who have been denied access to the means of representation, the photographer inevitably functions as an agent of the system of power that silenced these people in the first place. Thus, they are twice victimized: first by society, and then by the photographer who presumes the right to speak on their behalf.[13]

Gaskell is certainly guilty of presuming to speak on behalf of the workers of Manchester. But it would be too simple to conclude that her work was just an agent of prevailing systems of power: it caused too much controversy in her own class for that. In Gaskell's view, to speak for the self would be wrong, and public speech, especially in a woman, is fully justified only when it is speech on others' behalf. Her effort to record truthfully what she had heard succeeded to the extent that she made her rebellious workers more convincing than her narrative explanations, and seemed to many of her acquaintances to have betrayed her own class. Without her aim of speaking for others, Gaskell would probably not have been able to develop her own voice as a writer. For all her privileged class position, as a woman she clearly felt some fears of the indecor-ousness of women's public speaking, as dramatised in the trauma of Mary's behaviour at the trial. She overcame her fears, as Mary overcomes her inhibitions, by the thought that she was speaking for others. Hedged in by fears of the selfishness of self-expression, she needed the spur of an unselfish motive.[14] She applauds her characters, who, however oppressed themselves, always speak out for others; and by speaking for them in her turn, she emulates them.

3 Improper Women: *Ruth* and *The Life of Charlotte Brontë*

'I think I must be an improper woman without knowing it, I do so manage to shock people', wrote Gaskell to Eliza Fox early in 1853.

> Now *should* you have burned the 1st vol. of Ruth as so *very* bad? even if you had been a very anxious father of a family? yet *two* men have: and a third has forbidden his wife to read it; they sit next to us in Chapel and you can't think how 'improper' I feel under their eyes. (*L* 223)

Her anxious remark reveals a lot about the treatment of female sexuality and female knowledge in patriarchal culture. Men as fathers and husbands try to control what women may know, keeping from wives and from daughters the forbidden knowledge that might threaten their proper sexual behaviour and thus their status as men's property. In this case it is Gaskell's story of an unmarried mother that has been judged 'improper', particularly the first volume which depicts Ruth living with her seducer Bellingham. As her creator, Gaskell feels included in the disapproval of her heroine's impropriety, especially as the sinfulness of Ruth's life of sin is not at all points made clear.

Gaskell's defence – that she did not know she was being improper – is the crux of her attempt to deal with the problem. Woman's impropriety is of major importance to Gaskell: it is the central focus of *Ruth*, and is also, I shall argue, the underlying main concern of Gaskell's biography, *The Life of Charlotte Brontë*. In *Ruth* she deals with impropriety as sexual irregularity; in the biography of Brontë, with the related impropriety of a woman writer's expression of the 'coarse', a Victorian code-word for forbidden (to women) sexual knowledge. In each case her defence is that the accused, Ruth or Charlotte Brontë, did not know she was being improper: ignorant, therefore innocent.

Ruth was written out of a moral impulse similar to the one that generated *Mary Barton*: to make the middle-class reading public aware of responsibilities that they preferred to ignore. The story was controversial not simply because it was a story of seduction: that was an old and common theme (though in this period many novelists, like Dickens, feeling the pressure of having to produce safe family reading, trod extremely delicately whenever they introduced it), but because of the way Gaskell treated it. The seduced woman is no mere minor figure but the heroine, and Gaskell deliberately avoids treating seduction as a focus for easy pathos. It is not a 'fall' after which a woman can only sink lower or die of shame, but a mistake that given the chance she can outgrow. Gaskell focuses on the chance. The Dissenting minister Thurstan Benson finds Ruth pregnant and abandoned. What should he do? He and his sister Faith offer a home to her and her child, and find Ruth employment as a governess in the respectable Bradshaw family. The implication that this is how society should treat a 'fallen' woman shocked many readers. One reviewer explained:

We would open every door to the penitent woman –
we would . . . *woo her* back to virtue; we would
soothe her, and employ her, but we would not place
her as a teacher in a family – there is something
revolting in such communion between the maiden
girl and the spotted woman.[1]

Just how a woman could be welcomed, soothed, and
virtuously employed while being kept isolated from all
unspotted members of her sex is a problem
conveniently ignored here. Gaskell faced it, giving her
own version of the relationship between a maiden girl
and a spotted woman in the friendship between
Jemima Bradshaw and Ruth Hilton. Jemima, initially
horrified when she finds out about Ruth's past, learns
to appreciate that Ruth's present goodness is not
cancelled out by past mistakes, and that she herself has
been kept 'unspotted' by a careful upbringing and not
through any inherently greater purity. Jemima, far from
being corrupted by her contact with Ruth, is made a
better Christian by it; and through this and other
instances of Ruth's influence Gaskell shows the difference between her attitude to the 'fallen' and the
prevailing attitude in bourgeois society. She is not
arguing for pity for the sinner but for full acceptance.
One problem for Gaskell is that the chance she
engineers for Ruth must be based on deceit: only by
passing as a widow can Ruth be accepted in Eccleston.
This need not have mattered, and could in fact have
provided the opportunity for some cutting satire, had
she been intending to highlight the hypocrisy of
prevailing mores by showing that they forced deceit
onto anyone who opened doors to sinners. But Gaskell

is committed to the belief that it is wrong to do evil that good may come, and as narrator she provides unequivocal condemnation of Thurstan Benson's crucial decision to lie about Ruth. All through the time of Ruth's life as 'Mrs Denbigh' there are recurrent reminders of the falseness and insecurity of her position. Sally, the Benson's clear-headed if narrow-minded servant, is often employed to show events in a different perspective: she immediately sees through the story of Ruth's widowhood, and years later when Mr Benson decides to whip Leonard for lying, she reminds him in no uncertain terms that he has no right to punish the boy for that particular offence. Ruth's real rehabilitation into the community comes only after she has been exposed and vilified, and has proved her goodness by nursing many of the town's inhabitants through an epidemic. Gaskell's clear moral intention is to show the necessity of facing up to the truth; of accepting shame and then going beyond it.

However, she never provides a satisfactory answer to the defence of lying she gives to Faith Benson, once Ruth's past has been revealed. 'Ruth has had some years of peace, in which to grow stronger and wiser, so that she can bear her shame now in a way she never could have done at first . . . our telling a lie has been the saving of her' (R 361–2). Thurstan replies that they should have trusted to God, and told the truth – but the whole moral force of the novel lies in its indictment of Gaskell's society for making it so dangerous to be truthful about a woman's sexual irregularity. Faith Benson, in fact, has rather enjoyed deceiving people, cheerfully embroidering stories about Ruth's non-existent husband: 'I do think I've a talent for fiction, it is so pleasant to invent, and make the incidents dovetail together: and after all, if we are to tell a lie, we may as well do it thoroughly, or else it's of no use'

(150). Her enjoyment is clearly related to her creator's enjoyment in writing novels; and perhaps something of Gaskell's uneasiness about the morality of fiction-making surfaces here. Certainly she was particularly concerned, in *Ruth*, to avoid melodrama and write as soberly and truthfully as possible: wanting very much to do good by fiction, but perhaps not sure that it was possible after all.

There is the hint of an excuse for the lie about Ruth that is never made explicit: perhaps there has been no real untruth involved because Ruth is essentially, though not technically, the innocent woman she pretends to be. This seems to be implied in the episode in which Sally cuts Ruth's hair. A woman's long, flowing hair is a conventional symbol of her sexuality. Sally, ostensibly intending to make Ruth pass more easily as a widow, is really punishing her for being a sexual woman and banishing her sexuality from the Benson household. Ruth's meekness under this punishment first draws Sally to her and makes for the beginnings of real affection between them: it shows that Ruth is willing to renounce her sexuality and is therefore in a sense innocent after all. But Gaskell never makes the more radical claim that Thomas Hardy was to make forty years later in *Tess of the d'Urbervilles*, that the seduced woman can still be a pure woman without discounting her sexuality. On the innocence or guilt of her seduced heroine, Gaskell is uncomfortably equivocal.

Many contemporary readers felt that the novel was flawed because Ruth was made too innocent. She seems to have picked up no knowledge of sex from the gossip in the dressmaker's where she serves her apprenticeship.[2] In her early walks with Bellingham she cannot think why she feels uneasy about the pleasure she takes in his company; and when, sacked by her mistress for being seen with him, she agrees to go to London with Mr Bellingham, she seems unaware that any sexual proposition is involved. We next meet her in Wales, living happily with him, and it is not until a little boy calls her a naughty lady that she even seems to realise that there is anything irregular about the relationship. This may make her a more appealing heroine, reasoned Gaskell's contemporaries, but it spoils the argument for better treatment of seduced women, which must rest on typical, not exceptional cases. 'Ruth is no type of [the] class [of seduced women]'.[3] Again, that is Gaskell's point: to make people stop thinking of 'fallen women' as a class made up of certain types, who could be classified and provided with Magdalen houses and forgotten about, but as real individual women who need a place here and now. She does, however, reproduce one stereotype of the seduced maiden when she anxiously insists on the mitigating circumstances: Ruth is unguided, isolated and motherless.

It was the voice of outraged respectability that terrified Gaskell; but the criticisms that seem most forceful now came from the other side. Sympathetic readers felt that she had not gone far enough. For Ruth to die at the end, even with the admiration of the whole community, pandered to the notion that a seduced woman's fate must be tragic after all. 'Why should she die?' protested Charlotte Brontë.[4] Arthur Hugh Clough's comment is particularly illuminating; he objected not to Ruth's death but her penitence. He found the novel 'really very good, but it *is* a little too timid . . . I do not think that such overpowering humiliation should be the result in the soul of the not *really guilty*, though misguided girl'.[5] This pinpoints a central contradiction in the work: first Gaskell minimises Ruth's guilt, then writes approvingly of her excessive repentance. The core of Gaskell's problem here is the clash within her work of two attitudes to sexuality: one, almost Blakean, that it is natural and innocent, the other that (like other beauties of nature) it is part of a fallen world, and must be renounced in favour of a higher law.

The presentation of Ruth's relationship with Bellingham contains a good deal to offend Gaskell's pious neighbours. Sexual desire appears in a very positive light, explicitly approved when Bellingham's comfortable life of empty pettiness is interrupted by his meeting with Ruth, 'and a new, passionate, hearty feeling shot through his whole being' (33), implicitly valued through a series of associations between Ruth's responses to nature and her awakening sexual feelings. Her Sunday walks with Bellingham, virtually her only respite from long hours confined in the dressmaker's workshop, are full of images associating natural growth with tenderness and joy. Ruth's 'delight at the new tender beauty of an early spring day in February' (40), leads in the following months to longer walks, culminating in the visit to her old home after which her employer dismisses her and she goes to London with Bellingham. On this occasion, wandering through the countryside, Ruth stops 'in breathless delight' to look at a wooded plain 'tinted by the young tender hues of the earliest summer' (52), and despite vague moral warnings from her family's former servant, 'the newborn summer was so delicious that, in common with all young creatures, she shared its influence and was glad' (51). In scenes like this the young woman's sexual feelings are projected onto the landscape, and after Ruth's seduction she is shown responding to the Welsh scenery in a way that suggests correspondences between this and what cannot openly be discussed: her sexual relationship with Bellingham.

> In this manner they settled down to a week's enjoyment of that Alpine country. It was most true enjoyment to Ruth. It was opening a new sense; vast ideas of beauty and grandeur filled her mind at the sight of the mountains now first beheld in full majesty. She was almost overpowered by the vague and solemn delight. (65)

That her physical relationship with Bellingham is happy is suggested by a passage describing their harmony together in a beautiful green hollow of the Welsh woods, which has been praised as 'almost Lawrentian' in its ability to express sensuality through natural imagery.[6] In this and other scenes implying the naturalness and joyfulness of the couple's relationship, it does seem that Gaskell's imaginative sympathy is 'at odds with the preconceived moral purpose';[7] and her shocked neighbours were perhaps more perceptive readers than she liked to acknowledge.

Alongside this positive valuation of nature runs from the start a series of allusions to higher, ultimately religious, values. When Bellingham saves a child from drowning, this act of instinctive humanity is contrasted to the unattractive behaviour that takes over as soon as the child is placed in a social context: he is disgusted by the boy's dirty home and speaks superciliously to his grandmother. The narrative comments on Ruth's excessive admiration of him at this point:

> His spirited and natural action of galloping into the water to save the child, was magnified by Ruth into the most heroic deed of daring; his interest about the boy was tender, thoughtful benevolence in her eyes, and his careless liberality of money was fine generosity; for she forgot that generosity implies some degree of self-denial. (27–8)

Spirit and nature are not enough without the Christian virtue of self-denial. For all the delight in nature expressed in the early chapters there is no doubt about the speciousness of Bellingham's appeal to natural goodness when he suggests that Ruth comes with him: 'what is more natural (and, being natural, more right) than that you should throw yourself upon the care of the one who loves you dearly' (57). In Gaskell's moral world the liaison with Bellingham is natural and therefore the source of beauty and joy; but not therefore right.

Nature is not, however, simply opposed to and inferior to the moral and spiritual. In the Welsh scenes in particular Nature is a Wordsworthian teacher, expanding Ruth's imaginative sympathies and her spiritual capacities. Bellingham's merely physical enjoyment of Ruth's beauty and the beauties of nature contrasts with her soulful and self-forgetful response to the world. Walking out alone in the morning 'she knew not if she moved or stood still, for the grandeur of this beautiful earth absorbed all idea of separate and individual existence' (65). Ruth's repeatedly invoked capacity for self-forgetfulness is a measure of a moral stature far greater than Bellingham's; unlike him she can ultimately achieve the self-denial so central to Gaskell's ethics. Yet, ironically, it is what makes her vulnerable to seduction. It is because she forgets herself as she wanders, Eve-like, in 'natural, graceful, wavy lines' through the garden, 'careless of watchful eyes, indeed unconscious, for the time, of their existence' (49–50), that she fails to register old Thomas's biblical warning, and 'falls'. This same self-forgetfulness makes her love for Bellingham valuable, while his for her is simply selfish and sensual.

Yet the contrast Gaskell is drawing between mere sensual passion, and a love that, though illicit, shows

Ruth's capacity for spiritual goodness, is undermined by the sensuality of the very self-forgetfulness that indicates her spiritual potential. Bellingham the seducer is in fact remarkably lacking in sensuality in the Welsh scenes: bored and listless, he will not go out in the rain and cannot think of anything more exciting than card games to pass an evening. All the sensuality of description is given to Ruth's encounter with the natural world outside. His irritation with Ruth's delight in the scenery expresses his lack, in Romantic terms, of a heart capable of loving Nature; and in sexual terms, his inability to deal with the passionate human nature he has aroused. Before the seduction he had responded sexually with 'admiration' of Ruth's 'glowing, animated face', when a beautiful evening stirred her to joy; afterwards, Ruth's passionate responses bore him. It is the conventional message of seduction stories, that men tire of their conquests, presented in a way that emphasises less male perfidiousness than the weakness of his desire. The trouble with Bellingham is not just that he is sensual without being spiritual but that he is not sensual enough. Unable to sustain passion, he develops a fever that Gaskell brings in to resolve the situation. This breakdown delivers him into the hands of his mother, who once again takes over his life and reduces him to a whining but obedient boy, who turns away from passion and goes back to the boredom of his previous existence.

Ruth's moral superiority and her passionate nature are therefore linked, a subversive implication that Gaskell can only put forward with the excuse of Ruth's lack of self-consciousness. This aspect of self-forgetfulness is paradoxically both the sign of moral vulnerability (unthinking, unknowing, Ruth falls) and of moral capacity: to forget self is the first of virtues for

Gaskell, to be overly conscious of self a subtle yet
strong moral danger. Hence she puts Ruth, in danger of
seduction, in a contradictory moral position. Her first
excuse for Ruth's fateful Sunday walks is ignorance:
Ruth vaguely feels they are wrong, yet they are, 'as far
as reason and knowledge (*her* knowledge) went, so
innocent' (40). Ruth is acting (properly, on Unitarian
principles) from reason and knowledge, but unfortu-
nately her knowledge of sexual danger is very limited;
she lacks, as Gaskell stresses several times, a mother's
guidance. But what could her mother have said?

> She was too young when her mother died to have
> received any cautions or words of advice respecting
> *the* subject of a woman's life – if, indeed, wise
> parents ever directly speak of what, in its depth and
> power, cannot be put into words – which is a
> brooding spirit with no definite form or shape that
> men should know it, but which is there, and present
> before we have recognized and realized its existence.
> Ruth was innocent and snow-pure. She had heard of
> falling in love, but she did not know the signs and
> symptoms thereof; nor, indeed, had she troubled her
> head much about them. (44)

The contradictions in this important passage have been
pointed out.[8] Ruth falls because she has not been told
of sexuality, but she could not have been told, because
it is unnameable; Gaskell does not name it here. Yet it is
'*the* subject of a woman's life', its power increased by
the mystification of being unnameable, and the
religious connotations of the language used to refer to
it: 'a brooding spirit with no definite form or shape that
men should know it'. Ruth's purity consists of not
knowing, not troubling her head, about love and its

signs, not in not feeling it. The unnameable but all-important subject, the shapeless spirit, is present (in everyone, the choice of pronoun implies) without our knowledge. Ruth has sexual feelings but is unconscious of them. It is a sign of the challenge *Ruth* offered to the Victorian demarcation of female sexuality (according to which a woman is either normal and passionless, or an abnormal 'nymphomaniac') that Ruth's passionate nature troubles the moral scheme of the novel so much, and needs so insistently to be repressed.

Ruth's love for her illegitimate son Leonard is the main redeeming influence in her life: thus Gaskell explicitly opposes the morality that would consider a bastard tainted by its parents' sin. An early conversation between Faith and Thurstan Benson makes the point, Faith conventionally considering the child to be born to Ruth a 'badge of her shame', Thurstan calling it 'God's messenger to lead her back to Him' (119). The story of Leonard's birth and childhood show him to be right. Ruth, crucially, forgets herself in her child, and her responsibility for him leads unconsciously to her own moral and intellectual growth. She comes to realise, as she had not while she lived with him, Bellingham's shortcomings, and when Thurstan Benson offers her an intellectual education she learns quickly all that he can teach, so as to become in time her son's teacher: 'she did not think of herself at all, but of her boy, and what she must learn in order to teach him to be and to do as suited her hope and her prayer' (187).

Maternal love is a feeling Gaskell can afford to praise explicitly, and which she sentimentalises. As described in the novel it grows out of sexual love and is a means of escaping it. When Leonard is a baby Ruth is able to feel and acknowledge 'a strange yearning kind of love for the father of the child whom she pressed to her heart, which came, and she could not bid it begone as sinful, it was so pure and natural, even when thinking of it, as in the sight of God' (191); but at the same time she is haunted by dreams of her child becoming like his father. When Bellingham re-enters the novel as Mr Donne, the new candidate for Eccleston, Ruth's love for him is at first revived, and again vividly conveyed through natural imagery, this time drawn from the sea and sand at Abermouth, scene of their first reunion and of Ruth's final rejection of him. The renewed desire aroused by Mr Donne is subdued by her perception of his present selfishness, carelessness and corruption, which make it imperative to her to protect Leonard from his influence. Maternal love saves her from temptation.

Still, there is some ambivalence expressed about this 'natural', 'holy' feeling, as there is about sexual desire. Leonard's birth is announced in these terms: 'The earth was still "hiding her guilty front with innocent snow," when a little baby was laid by the side of the pale white mother' (160). Pale Ruth, figuratively linked to the earth as mother, shares its guilty front: an unmarried mother passing herself off as a widowed one, she is guilt masquerading as innocence. The quotation, from Milton's 'Ode on the morning of Christ's Nativity', has a complex message: it simultaneously suggests links between Leonard's illegitimate birth and the virgin birth of Christ, thus offering a challenging affirmation of the holiness of life; and it recalls the concept of a fallen humanity, a guilty earth, that needs the redemption offered by Christ. Ruth hopes to shield her child from sin, and Gaskell, with gentle irony, suggests the impossibility of doing so: 'And *her* mother had thought the same, most probably' (161). Faith warns the new mother not to make an idol of her child. The narrative comment on Ruth's response is warmer about mother love, but does not discount the warning:

'[Ruth's] internal voice whispered that God was "Our Father", and that he knew our frame, and knew how natural was the first outburst of a mother's love; so, although she treasured up the warning, she ceased to affright herself for what had already gushed forth' (162). Mother love is given great power in this novel, but it is in the end subordinated to love of 'Our Father'.

Ruth's death at the end of the novel seems to me less of a sop to the conventional notion that female sexual transgression must lead to death, than a result of Gaskell's fundamental ambivalence about the value of the intense maternal devotion that, in Ruth's life, has absorbed all her sexual feelings. She tries not to smother Leonard with protective love as he grows older, but it is hard for her; hard to leave him for any length of time, hard to agree to the doctor's suggestion of taking the adolescent boy on as an apprentice. Her death seems contrived to free him from the possibly stultifying effects of her affection (we have already seen, in Bellingham's relation with his mother, the undesirable effect of a mother's too exclusive attachment to her son). The immediate cause of Ruth's death, however, is the remnant of her love for Bellingham/ Donne: she is attracted to him no longer, except when the treacherous helplessness of fever allows love to express itself as tender compassion. She cannot resist the desire to nurse him. And while she has nursed a townful of diseased people in apparent immunity to infection, the fever from which her former lover recovers is fatal to her. The sexual and emotional tangle in the mind of Gaskell's sinful, saintly heroine is escaped by returning her to unconsciousness: she lies on her death-bed 'softly gazing at vacancy with her open, unconscious eyes, from which all the depth of their meaning had fled, and all they told of was of a

sweet, child-like insanity within' (448). She is returned
to innocence and ignorance in death.

At the same time that Gaskell was getting ready to
publish *Ruth*, Charlotte Brontë was preparing *Villette*
for the press; but the latter delayed the publication of
her novel to give her friend's work first chance with
the reviewers. Brontë wanted to avoid comparisons
between her own novel and *Ruth*: 'not that I think that
she . . . would suffer from contact with "Villette" – we
know not but that the damage might be the other
way', she explained.[9] It was; at least, so it appeared
in the long and extremely favourable review that
J. M. Ludlow wrote for the *North British Review* in May
1853. After praising Gaskell for taking 'her calling as
an author in Christian earnest' and suggesting that
women's natures especially fitted them for doing God's
work in novels, Ludlow went on to divide women
writers on the basis of marital status:

> when we look at female writers, we cannot help
> being struck by the vast superiority of the married,
> as a class, over the single . . . *the* woman's book of
> the age – 'Uncle Tom's Cabin' – is that of a wife and
> a mother; and even if we contrast the two names
> more immediately before us, those of the authoresses
> of 'Jane Eyre' and 'Mary Barton', many of us at least
> can hardly repress the feeling, that the works of the
> former, however more striking in point of intellect,
> have in them a something harsh, rough, unsatisfying,
> some say all but unwomanly, as compared to the full,
> and wholesome, and most womanly perfection of the
> other.[10]

A footnote made explicit reference to *Villette* as even
worse than Brontë's earlier works: 'unequal',

'imperfect' and 'constantly untrue to itself and to her own great powers'. From the general comments on women writers, two objections that apply to *Villette* emerge. Brontë's novel deals with love, a subject on which, in Ludlow's view, unmarried women could produce either incompetent writing born of in-experience, or immodest work born of reprehensible knowledge. By implication, a novel concentrating so reprehensibly on the writer's presumably bitter personal experience must neglect the Christian calling to write for others' good.

This criticism of Brontë for (almost) unwomanliness echoed a strain that had been heard in the reception of her work all along. There was certainly genuine and generous recognition of the power of her work from *Jane Eyre* onwards, but there were also always those who discerned something subversive in her tone, from Elizabeth Rigby's *Quarterly Review* article, finding in *Jane Eyre* the kind of spirit that led to Chartism and revolution, and claiming that only a man or a depraved woman 'who had long ago for sufficient reason forfeited the society of her own sex' could have written it, to Matthew Arnold's pronouncement that 'hunger, rebellion and rage' filled *Villette*.[11]

Brontë was well aware that her work did not have the philanthropic credentials of a novel like Harriet Beecher Stowe's *Uncle Tom's Cabin*: much as she honoured philanthropy, she wrote to George Smith, she could not emulate such a work: '"Villette" touches on no matter of public interest. I cannot write books handling the topics of the day; it is of no use trying. Nor can I write a book for its moral.' To Gaskell she wrote: '"Villette" has indeed no right to push itself before "Ruth". There is a goodness, a philanthropic purpose, a social use in the latter, to which the former cannot for an instant pretend'.[12] *Villette* has no seduced heroine, no illegitimacy, no open challenge to the double standard. Its heroine Lucy Snowe lives a quiet and blameless life as a nurserymaid and then teacher. But she flouts Victorian womanly convention, less obviously but more profoundly than Ruth does, by being – shockingly for a heroine – cold, and to many readers, unlikeable; she casts a sardonic eye on the more womanly women of her narrative. Worst of all, her coldness is the effect of a passionate nature sternly repressed: her narrative reveals the passion underneath, the tortured attraction she feels towards both John Graham Bretton and Paul Emanuel. Lucy's description of her own self-division, when stern Reason and seductive Imagination play out her inner drama, show her to be anything but the unconscious innocent. Her introspection and self-analysis are diametrically opposed to the unreflective, outward-looking goodness that is Gaskell's ideal.

Villette was written out of the imperative to express personal suffering, without a morally useful aim: most of Brontë's contemporaries would agree that it touched on no matter of public interest. Looking back now, though, we can see that it dealt with, precisely, a topic of the day that the day was studiously ignoring: a matter that was not considered to be of public interest because it concerned women's private feelings. In a society where woman's destiny was supposed to be marriage and children, how was an unmarried woman like Lucy Snowe supposed to feel? There was plenty of discussion of the need for work to provide her with economic support and a purpose in life; but it was a different matter to acknowledge in her feelings of alienation, of sexual desire or of anger, to suggest that such feelings lived beneath the coolest and most proper of exteriors. *Villette* does this, and so it offended not just conservative beliefs about woman's place but the

assumptions of Victorian feminism. Brontë's friendship
with the feminist Harriet Martineau split on the rock of
Villette. 'All the female characters, in all their thoughts
and lives, are full of one thing, or are regarded by the
reader in the light of that one thought, – love',
protested Martineau. 'There are substantial, heartfelt
interests for women of all ages, and under ordinary
circumstances, quite apart from love.' That is the very
necessary voice of nineteenth-century feminism, insist-
ing on woman's right to be considered as more than a
vessel of emotion. Important moves to improve
women's education, job opportunities and property
rights were made because of that voice. Yet Charlotte
Brontë made an important, if unintentional, con-
tribution to feminism because she had to say what that
voice had to suppress. 'There is an absence of introspection, an unconsciousness, a repose in women's
lives', claimed Martineau, attacking *Villette* and de-
fending women as reasonable nineteenth-century
creatures.[13] There is not, claims Brontë's novel, or if
there is it is the effect of a dangerous inner repression.
Villette is profoundly subversive of the Victorian belief
in good womanhood.

Gaskell was aware that the so-called coarseness and
naughtiness of Brontë's novels arose from an honesty
about the self that she deeply admired and could not
quite achieve.

> The difference between Miss Brontë and me is that
> she puts all her naughtiness into her books, and I put
> all my goodness. I am sure she works off a great deal
> that is morbid *into* her writing, and *out* of her life;
> and my books are so far better than I am that I often
> feel ashamed of having written them and as if I were
> a hypocrite. (*L* 228)

Brontë discerned something of this too, writing to Gaskell, apropos of *Ruth*,

> Do you, who have so many friends – so large a circle of acquaintance – find it easy, when you sit down to write, to isolate yourself from all those ties, and their sweet associations, so as to be quite *your own woman*, uninfluenced unswayed by the consciousness of how your work may affect other minds; what blame, what sympathy it may call forth? Does no luminous cloud ever come between you and the severe Truth as you know it in your own secret and clear-seeing soul?[14]

Brontë told Gaskell not to answer this question; perhaps she knew the answer already. Gaskell did sometimes let clouds obscure the truths she knew, and never more so, ironically, than in the biography of Brontë herself.

Gaskell, as we have seen (ch. 1, p. 22), was delighted by the favourable reception of *Ruth* in the *North British Review*, but she was troubled by the article's slurs on unmarried women writers in general and Brontë in particular. No doubt she remembered Brontë's determination that no invidious comparisons between *Ruth* and *Villette* should split the friends: 'they *shall* not make us foes; they *shall* not mingle with our mutual feelings one taint of jealousy: there is my hand on that: I know you will return clasp for clasp'.[15] She found out who had written the anonymous article and let J. M. Ludlow know that not all unmarried women writers had the faults he described: 'I should like to tell you a good deal about Miss Brontë – & her wild sad life . . . and after all she is so much better, & more faithful than her books'.[16] It was a foretaste of the campaign that began in earnest after Brontë's death.

The Life of Charlotte Brontë says rather little about the

novels: there is general trumpeting of *Jane Eyre*, 'laid high and safe on the everlasting hills of fame', and a refusal to go further: 'I am not going to write an analysis of a book with which everyone who reads this biography is sure to be acquainted' (*LCB* 326). Indeed, Gaskell's original reactions to *Jane Eyre* had been equivocal: 'I don't know whether I like or dislike it' she had written (*L* 57). That was before she knew its author. Whereas Gaskell's deep admiration for George Eliot's writing forced her to like the novelist in spite of the liaison with G. H. Lewes, in Charlotte Brontë's case it was her love for the woman that made her admire the writings. In *The Life* she is concerned to present the woman, as good daughter, sister and eventually wife. A woman, argues Gaskell, enlarging on the theme that had exercised her before, can write without neglecting a woman's proper duties. Cleverly she turned Robert Southey's contrary opinion to good use. 'Literature cannot be the business of a woman's life, and it ought not to be. The more she is engaged in her proper duties, the less leisure will she have for it, even as an accomplishment and a recreation', he had written (*LCB* 173). Gaskell points out the potentially disastrous effects of such a pronouncement from the Poet Laureate to a young writer: 'This "stringent" letter made her put aside, for a time, all idea of literary enterprise' (176). At the same time she insists that Charlotte Brontë found it an admirable letter. It was only by admiring it that she could prove it wrong. Charlotte Brontë replied to Southey, 'I have endeavoured not only attentively to observe all the duties a woman ought to fulfil, but to feel deeply interested in them' (175), and Gaskell corroborated this claim throughout her biography. No household duty, no call for womanly sympathy, she insisted, was neglected in the service of Brontë's artistic vision. She might be completely possessed by creative inspiration, but she would find time secretly to peel the potatoes that the ailing servant Tabby had not managed to deal with properly, thus combining fastidious housekeeping with delicate attention to others' feelings (306). This is one example of the 'double life' that is Gaskell's implied answer to Southey and her defence of the woman writer, formulated in the biography:

> Henceforward Charlotte Brontë's existence becomes divided into two parallel currents – her life as Currer Bell, the author; her life as Charlotte Brontë, the woman. There were separate duties belonging to each character – not opposing each other; not impossible, but difficult to be reconciled. . . . a woman's principal work in life is hardly left to her own choice; nor can she drop the domestic charges devolving on her as an individual, for the exercise of the most splendid talents that were ever bestowed. And yet she must not shrink from the extra responsibility implied by the very fact of her possessing such talents. She must not hide her gift in a napkin; it was meant for the use and service of others. (334)

It sounds as much a defence of Elizabeth Gaskell as of Charlotte Brontë, and the justification by writing's altruistic purpose would have suited Brontë less than it did Gaskell.

Gaskell's defence of Brontë, then, was in terms of Victorian womanliness rather than in terms of the special qualities of her writing. Gaskell does appeal to Brontë's 'strong feeling of the duty of representing life as it really is, not as it ought to be' (496), but she regards it as a matter of blame (others', not Charlotte Brontë's) that Brontë knew life as it is, and stresses as far as possible her subject's innocence and unconsciousness. She emphasises 'how utterly unconscious she was of what was, by some, esteemed coarse in her writing', and she describes how shocked Brontë was to hear *Jane Eyre* called a 'naughty book'; in a manner reminiscent of the excuses for *Ruth*, she makes the loss of a mother's guidance significant, drawing a pathetic scene in which Brontë asks Mrs Smith 'as she would have asked a mother – if she had not been motherless from early childhood' what was wrong in *Jane Eyre* (495). The coarseness that Gaskell acknowledges to be in Brontë's work is all the fault of men: the few men she knew are accused of talking 'before her, if not to her, with as little reticence as Rochester talked to Jane Eyre', and her 'poor brother's sad life' of drunkenness, opium addiction and adulterous love is the source for Brontë's unfortunate knowledge of evil: 'circumstances forced her to touch pitch, as it were, and by it her hand was for a moment defiled. It was but skin-deep' (496).

If men, especially her brother Branwell, are blamed for much of Brontë's suffering and apparent un-womanliness, it is a woman who is the ultimate scapegoat of the book. In 1845 Branwell was dismissed from his post as tutor in the Robinson household; it was said that he was having an affair with his employer's wife. According to Gaskell, Branwell remained hopelessly in love with Mrs Robinson, and when, after her husband's death, she refused to see her lover again, afraid of losing the fortune left con-ditionally to her, his despair led to his rapid decline and death. Gaskell descends into cliché as she describes the advances of this 'mature and wicked woman', to whose love Branwell so mistakenly trusted, for 'he little knew how bad a depraved woman can be' (273, 283). Not only Branwell's death but his sisters' deaths (hastened by grief) are 'in part' blamed on this 'profligate woman' who 'goes flaunting about to this day in respectable society; a showy woman for her age;

kept afloat by her reputed wealth. I see her name in county papers, as one of those who patronize the Christmas balls; and I hear of her in London drawing-rooms' (281). No wonder Mrs Robinson (by this time Lady Scott) threatened the author of *The Life of Charlotte Brontë* with legal action.

Gaskell's intention was to tell the truth and to speak out fearlessly against vice, but it certainly seems that in her eagerness to blame Mrs Robinson she wandered into fiction: Mr Robinson's will did not contain the clause Gaskell mentions, disinheriting his widow if she saw Branwell Brontë again.[17] One reason she is so keen to heap blame on Mrs Robinson is that it allows her to deflect attention from anything people might have found blameworthy in her heroine. Gaskell was aware of Charlotte Brontë's passionate and unrequited love for Constantin Heger, who with his wife ran the school in Brussels attended by Charlotte and Emily Brontë. Gaskell had visited Brussels, met the Hegers, read Brontë's letters to Heger, and was aware that the relationship between Lucy Snowe and Paul Emanuel in *Villette* was partly based on Brontë's unhappy love. Here, exactly, was what detractors like J. M. Ludlow would have predicted: the unmarried woman writer was writing out of her own bitter experience, her own immodest desires. To have revealed anything of this, quite apart from the distress it would have caused the people concerned, would have ruined Gaskell's defence of her friend as a truly womanly writer. She chose to suppress it. The story of Branwell's downfall came in very handy. Suppression of the Heger story involved 'the ante-dating of Branwell's ruin – advanced by 18 months – to account for Charlotte's low spirits after her return from Brussels'.[18] Moreover, the presence of a scarlet woman in the narrative makes Brontë seem the purer. All the 'naughtiness' whose existence in

Charlotte Brontë Gaskell wanted to deny was projected onto this convenient target, magnified and denounced.

Gaskell, who elsewhere wrote so much that undermined conventional Victorian notions of womanhood, takes part here in the classic patriarchal division of womankind. Mrs Robinson takes the part of the depraved sexual woman, Charlotte Brontë that of the pure and innocent one. In her eagerness to present her friend as a woman her society would honour, Gaskell underestimated Brontë's fiction and wove fiction round Brontë's life. Like her own Faith Benson, she used fictional embroidery to create an image of innocence and unconsciousness for the woman whose cause she championed.

4 Changes: *Cranford* and *North and South*

Cranford (1851–3) and *North and South* (1854–5) in
many ways represent opposite poles of Gaskell's
achievement. *Cranford* is a humorous rendering of old-
fashioned life in a small rural town: mainly set (there
are a few minor inconsistencies in dating) in the 1830s,
and glancing back over its characters' histories as far as
the 1780s, it re-creates a quiet and quaint way of
genteel life that at first sight may appear static. The
action of *North and South* is undated but evidently
meant to be contemporary: it deals with the new
industrial town Milton, with the new class groupings
of industrial working class and capitalist manufacturer,
with the topical issue of strikes. Milton is young, harsh
and rapidly changing, its newness emphasised by
being experienced through the consciousness of
Margaret Hale, an unwilling emigrant from an older
way of life. Yet for all the difference in pace, both
works are concerned with social change. Life in
Cranford is in fact subject to change: personal losses are
often the focus of individual episodes, but the picture
emerging from the narrative as a whole is of beneficial
changes to the community. They differ from the
changes in *North and South* mainly by coming about
more gently and gradually.

Both works focus on a question that was always of
importance to Gaskell: what role can a woman take in
her changing society? The nervous, prematurely aged
Miss Matty Jenkyns could hardly be more of a contrast,

as heroine, to the energetic and positive Margaret Hale.
But for both of them the question of a single woman's
agency arises. When the Town and County Bank fails,
leaving Miss Matty, in her fifties, faced with the
prospect of having to earn her own living, the narrator
Mary Smith wonders 'what in the world Miss Matty
could do' (CCP 186). Teaching is the obvious first
thought, but Miss Matty does not even have ladies'
accomplishments, never mind learning. A summary of
her practical abilities comes down to making candle-
lighters and knitting garters. Mary Smith concludes:

> No! there was nothing she could teach to the rising
> generation of Cranford; unless they had been quick
> learners and ready imitators of her patience, her
> humility, her sweetness, her quiet contentment with
> all that she could not do. (CCP 186)

Miss Matty is the embodiment of a sentimental
feminine ideal much praised in the eighteenth century
into which she was born: being, not doing, is her forte,
and her virtues are all passive ones. She does in fact
have some success in contributing to her own support
from the sale of tea, but this commercial venture is
given up as soon as her long-lost brother Peter returns
from India with enough money for them to live 'very
genteelly' (209), which means that Matty can give up
trying to do anything and concentrate on simply being
a force for 'peace and kindliness'. 'We all love Miss
Matty, and I somehow think we are all of us better
when she is near us' concludes Mary Smith (218), on a
sugary note that the narrative, with its careful blend of
humour and pathos, usually manages to avoid.

Margaret Hale, in contrast, is always active: single-
ness, to her, when late in the novel she is left parentless
and suddenly rich, means freedom and responsibility.

> She had learnt . . . that she herself must one day
> answer for her own life, and what she had done with
> it; and she tried to settle that most difficult problem
> for women, how much was to be utterly merged in
> obedience to authority, and how much might be set
> apart for freedom in working. (NS 508)

She solves it easily enough, since authority is embodied
in her aunt Shaw, conventionally minded but weak-
willed, and easily charmed into agreement with Margaret's plans. Just what these plans are is left vague,
probably because by this stage of composition Gaskell
was running out of space. From Edith's remarks about
'the dirt you'll pick up in those places' (509), Margaret
is evidently engaged in some kind of philanthropic
work, an area into which Victorian middle-class women
were expanding their womanly sphere. We do not
really need further details, as this work is so clearly an
offshoot of the good works Margaret has been
performing for family and community throughout the
novel. What is important about the new duties is that
they require no fundamental change in her: to her
cousin Edith's fears that she will become dowdy and
strong-minded she responds,'I'm going to be just the
same, Edith, if you and my aunt could but fancy so.
Only as I have neither husband nor child to give me
natural duties, I must make myself some' (509).
    Singleness is never a desirable state in Gaskell, but
one to be made the best of: Miss Matty's life is seen as
a blighted one because she never marries and has
children, while Margaret's self-made duties occupy
only a brief interval before 'natural duties', in the shape
of marriage to Thornton, come to claim her love and
money. Gaskell thought 'an unmarried life may be to
the full as happy, *in process of time* but I think there is a
time of trial to be gone through with *women*, who

naturally yearn after children' (L 598), and both for
Miss Matty and Margaret Hale, children are a focus of
regret. Yet what they miss, and why, differs. Miss Matty
confesses:

> I dream sometimes that I have a little child – always
> the same – a little girl of about two years old; she
> never grows older, though I have dreamt about her
> for many years. I don't think I ever dream of any
> words or sound she makes; she is very noiseless and
> still, but she comes to me when she is very sorry or
> very glad, and I have wakened with the clasp of her
> dear little arms round my neck. (CCP 158–9)

Miss Matty's silent dream-child contrasts with Margaret's substitute for a child of her own. She excels in
looking after Edith's little boy when he is too
boisterous for his mother to handle:

> She would carry him off into a room, where they two
> alone battled it out; she with a firm power which
> subdued him into peace, while every sudden charm
> and wile she possessed, was exerted on the side of
> right, until he would rub his little hot and tear-
> smeared face all over hers, kissing and caressing till
> he often fell asleep in her arms or on her shoulder.
> Those were Margaret's sweetest moments. They gave
> her a taste of the feeling that she believed would be
> denied to her for ever. (NS 495)

For Margaret, love is most desirable as a battle in
which the woman's power is exerted on the side of
right, and her victory is to turn male aggression into
tenderness. This little scene indicates the effect she is to
have on Thornton, and by extension, the aggressive
masculine world of Milton-Northern. In Miss Matty,

femininity is a passive longing for love; in Margaret, woman's love is an active force that can change the world.

Both *Cranford* and *North and South* explore the effects of the split in society between private and public, rational and emotional, expressed in the notion of 'separate spheres' for men and women. Although their respective heroines are so different – Matty being a victim of the split, Margaret having the potential to begin healing it – both works address the split as a problem and both offer a fundamentally optimistic view of the possibilities of healing, through the extension of 'feminine' concern with nurturance into 'masculine' areas of life.

In *Cranford* the Victorian idea of separate spheres has been taken to extremes.[1] This is established in the first few sentences, which create the sense of an almost mythical world of feminine separatism, and also suggest its fragile basis.

> In the first place, Cranford is in possession of the Amazons; all the holders of houses, above a certain rent, are women. If a married couple come to settle in the town, somehow the gentleman disappears; he is either fairly frightened to death by being the only man in the Cranford evening parties, or he is accounted for by being with his regiment, his ship, or closely engaged in business all the week in the great neighbouring commercial town of Drumble, distant only twenty miles on a railroad. In short, whatever does become of the gentlemen, they are not at Cranford. (39)

Drumble is the place of masculine, public, commercial values, understood by no one in Cranford but close to it and linked by that nineteenth-century symbol of technological progress and the quickening pace of life, the railway. Financially dependent though the ladies of Cranford may be on the income from their small investments in that commercial world, they continue to live as if it did not exist. Deborah Jenkyns clings to the social status once accorded her as the rector's daughter, though the affluence that once went with her position has vanished since her father's death. Other Cranford ladies in similarly reduced circumstances also rely for self-respect on an exaggerated sense of rank and the importance of gentility, and do their best to ignore the fact that the nineteenth century is leaving them financially and socially behind. The humorous designation of the Cranford ladies as female warriors, and the mock-sinister reference to men being frightened to death, establish an undercurrent of hostility to men; but in the very first sentence, the phrase 'above a certain rent' alerts us to the fact that the disappearance of men is an illusion. In the lower classes, from which the ladies see themselves as quite distinct, there are, as the servant Martha later confirms, 'such lots of young fellows' that the town is a particularly good place for finding a husband (79). The Cranford ladies' separation from commercial life, from present-day society and from men is a kind of collective fantasy.

Because the Cranford ladies live so exclusively in the home, shopping and frequent visits to each others' houses being their main excursions, and because they do not share their homes with men, in their lives the woman's sphere seems to have expanded into an entire 'community of women', which Nina Auerbach has suggested appears in a very positive light as against the male-dominated public one.[2] Certainly Cranford's co-operative social ethos is cherished. Miss Matty, as a shareholder in the Town and County Bank, is right (though she goes against all commercial sense) to take on responsibility for the farmer's banknote when the bank fails; and her friends' subsequent rallying round to support her, and the local grocer's uncompetitive attitude, which helps ensure the success of her tea business, further vindicate Cranford in its opposition to Drumble. However, kindness and mutual help make up only one of the two sets of values associated with Cranford. The other, associated with Miss Deborah rather than Miss Matty, is the 'strict code of gentility' (*CCP* 109), which dictates the preservation of outmoded social distinctions. Both value systems can be associated with femininity. The Cranford ladies are responsible for the idea that gentility is feminine: they almost believe, reports Mary Smith, that 'to be a man [is] to be "vulgar"' (45). It is Victorian ideology that identifies kindly co-operation as a part of womanliness, opposed to masculine aggression. Gaskell is gently mocking the Cranford ladies' gentility, seeing it as the result not of femininity but the peculiar social situation of this group of women. Their kindness she whole-heartedly endorses, but does not attribute to women alone. Her aim is to show the 'separate spheres' of Cranford to be illusory, and to suggest that 'womanly' values can and should be shared by men and women. She neither sees Cranford as a separatist 'community of women' to be celebrated, nor, as Martin Dodsworth has suggested, as a world of sterile gentility that needs masculinisation.[3] Rather her vision is of a world of inevitable social change in which she hopes to preserve the best and discard the worst aspects of an earlier way of life.

Gaskell's attitude to the collective fantasies of Cranford combines amused indulgence and gentle, but telling criticism. It is well conveyed through her choice of narrator, Mary Smith: younger than the other ladies and spending some of her time in Drumble, she both includes herself in the Cranford 'we' and distances herself from it, seeing through 'our' self-deceptions even as she celebrates them. The principal of these is their refusal to acknowledge their own poverty, which indicates both their economic difficulties as women without men, and the decline of a social system in which aristocratic connections counted for more than commercial success. Thus Mrs Forrester, related to a 'good' family but now a poor widow, pretends, with her friends' connivance, that she is the leisured mistress of a household of servants, who does not know 'what cakes were sent up, though she knew, and we knew, and she knew that we knew, and we knew that she knew we knew, she had been busy all the morning making tea-bread and sponge cakes' (41). The tone here is indulgent because approval of the 'kindly *esprit de corps*' shown by the Cranford ladies outweighs any mockery of their fantasy of gentility. But when the code of gentility discourages kindness and co-operation it is criticised. As Miss Matty's past is gradually revealed, we realise that her father's and sister's standards of gentility denied her the chance to marry the farmer she loved; while in Cranford's present, Mrs Jamieson tries to exclude Mrs Fitz-Adam from the ladies' society because she was born a farmer's daughter. In fact, the social barriers so jealously preserved by Miss Deborah Jenkyns, and after her death by Mrs Jamieson, are already crumbling. Everyone else visits Mrs Fitz-Adam, and Mrs Jamieson is fittingly punished when her own sister-in-law (and the only titled lady in the book), Lady Glenmire, marries Mrs Fitz-Adam's brother, the surgeon Mr Hoggins. In *Cranford* Gaskell lovingly documents the quaintness of the town – its love of old lace washed in buttermilk, its old-fashioned red silk umbrellas – and also shows how this is bound up with its clinging to an

outmoded social structure. The ending, in which Mr
Peter enchants the naïve Cranford ladies with his tall
tales of India, and uses the authority thus gained in
the community to reconcile Mrs Jamieson and the
Hogginses, expresses a hope that Cranford quaintness
can somehow survive even as a new social order is
accepted.

Repeatedly, change is introduced into Cranford and
then absorbed, its threat defused by the revelation that
what seems foreign is in reality familiar and kind. This
is particularly evident in the treatment of a kind of sex
war between the Cranford ladies and a series of
'invading' men. Military associations and metaphors
suggest the war between masculine and feminine.
Captain Brown, Major Jenkyns and Major Gordon all
visit Cranford after a lifetime in the army, and Captain
Brown's arrival is seen by the Cranford ladies as 'the
invasion of their territories by a man and a gentleman'
(42). Many of the male characters have spent time in
'the East', particularly India, suggesting the foreignness
and the threat of masculinity in Cranford minds. Major
Jenkyns's 'Hindoo body-servant' who makes Miss
Matty think of the legendary wife-killer Bluebeard (68),
and the comparison of the visiting magician, Signor
Brunoni, to the 'Grand Turk' (135), a figure in the
European imagination for polygamy and male
domination, demonstrate that fear of men is displaced
onto fear of foreigners. The fears are consistently
shown to be groundless, the foreignness an illusion.
Captain Brown shatters Cranford fantasy by his
'vulgar' talk of poverty, but still he shares poverty with
them; he does take up a 'man's place' in the
community, but just like a woman's, it is a place of
service. At a Cranford card-party

He immediately and quietly assumed the man's

place in the room; attended to every one's wants,
lessened the pretty maid-servant's labour by waiting
on empty cups, and bread-and-butterless ladies; and
yet did it all in so easy and dignified a manner, and
so much as if it were a matter of course for the strong
to attend to the weak, that he was a true man
throughout. (46)

His manliness is defined in terms of service to family
and community – he is devoted to his daughters, helps
his neighbours and dies on the railway saving a little
girl. Although he is employed by the hated new railway, he is the victim, not the representative, of
technological and commercial progress. Thus he shares
with the Cranford ladies the best of their values and
their apparently 'feminine' vulnerability.

Captain Brown's death in the second number was
originally intended to end the series; and when Gaskell
decided to add episodes and eventually to develop
Cranford into a full narrative, she created new
disruptive masculine figures. The name of the most
important one echoes the captain's: Signor Brunoni,
alias Samuel Brown. The apparent threat of masculinity
is even stronger here: Signor Brunoni, it appears, really
is a foreigner, and has magical powers (it is Miss Pole,
the Cranfordian most openly hostile to men and
marriage, who insists he has merely learnt some easy
conjuring tricks); and his arrival coincides with a series
of robberies, some real and some imagined, which
place Cranford in a state of panic. The Cranford ladies
begin to blame this exotic man for their problems, Mrs
Forrester conflating various nationalities in her self-
protective fantasy that Cranford is a haven of goodness
and all threat must be foreign:

we must believe that the robbers were strangers – if

strangers, why not foreigners? – if foreigners, who so likely as the French? Signor Brunoni spoke broken English like a Frenchman, and, though he wore a turban like a Turk, Mrs Forrester had seen a print of Madame de Staël with a turban on, and another of Mr Denon in just such a dress as that in which the conjurer had made his appearance; showing clearly that the French, as well as the Turks, wore turbans: there could be no doubt Signor Brunoni was a Frenchman – a French spy, come to discover the weak and undefended places of England. (139)

Again, all fears are illusory. The robbery at Mr Hoggins's is reduced to a cat's theft of meat; the ladies' homes are quite safe; and there are no ghosts in Darkness-lane, which they so fear to enter at night. Signor Brunoni is mere Samuel Brown, once in the army in India, now a conjurer, and a poor, ill man with a wife and daughter. Miss Pole was right to doubt his power but wrong to be hostile towards him. Like other men in Cranford, he is as vulnerable as women: 'pale and feeble, and with his heavy filmy eyes, that only brightened a very little when they fell upon the countenance of his faithful wife, or their pale and sorrowful little girl' (155). India itself loses its foreign-ness as Mrs Brown tells her tale of walking through the country with her baby girl, and receiving kind assist-ance from Hindus like the one who had so frightened Miss Matty. She is also helped by 'Aga Jenkyns', who turns out to be Miss Matty's long-lost brother, so that the friendship with the apparently threatening Signor Brunoni becomes a means of effecting the final reunion of brother and sister.

The ending includes all kinds of reconciliation and the merging of differences. Peter Jenkyns, whose boyish pranks, both involving impersonating women, can be read as covert protests against the sharp divisions between men and women, returns to live with his sister, a reunion that symbolises Cranford's recognition of the kinship between the sexes. Matty also gains a family in Martha and Jem Hearn and their baby daughter, her godchild. Social divisions are being blurred here, as Martha, Matty's servant, is now her landlady; and Martha has always been a destroyer of social pretensions, shocking Cranford gentility by comparing Lady Glenmire to Mrs Deacon at the 'Coach and Horses' (117). The change should not be exaggerated: Martha still has the devoted-servant mentality and her husband Jem shows his deference by keeping out of Miss Matty's way. Gaskell is aiming to soften, not undermine, class distinction. But beneficial change is depicted in all aspects of Cranford society: different classes and the sexes have been reconciled, and the 'womanly' values of caring have proved themselves central to women's and men's experience.

Gaskell has had to leave certain things out to present this optimistic vision of gradual and beneficient social change. While *Mary Barton* and *North and South* deal with the confrontation between workers and capital, *Cranford* concentrates on healing the divisions between the 'aristocratic' and merely 'respectable' ends of the middle class. As she heals the division between men and women by implying that 'womanly' values are shared by all, she expels from Cranford any hint of the male violence that threatens women in the world outside her fable. Her Cranford ladies fear attacks that are never going to happen. Their covert antagonism towards men is quite unnecessary: men, when known, are as kindly and vulnerable as women. Interestingly, in 'The Last Generation in England', the essay that contained the original germ of *Cranford*, and which she

claimed to be a truthful account of country town life a
generation ago, Gaskell presented a different story:

> hanging on the outskirts of society were a set of
> young men, ready for mischief and brutality, and
> every now and then dropping off the pit's brink into
> crime. . . . They would stop ladies returning from the
> card-parties, which were the staple gaity of the place,
> and who were only attended by a maidservant
> bearing a lantern, and whip them; literally whip
> them as you whip a little child; until administering
> such chastisement to a good, precise old lady of high
> family, 'my brother, the magistrate', came forward
> and put down such proceedings with a high hand.
> (CCP 320)

This is an exemplary instance of male violence being
used as social control of women, who are clearly being
punished for having a social life independent of men;
and of men expressing class antagonism through
victimisation of the women of a higher class, forcing
them, in their turn, to rely on the class power wielded
by their men for protection. It would have badly
damaged the tone of Cranford to include anything like
this; instead, we have baseless fears of ghosts in
Darkness-lane. By repressing the acknowledgement of
threats to her female community, Gaskell is able to
present in Cranford a comforting myth in which men
and women, and different classes, do not really have
conflicting interests, and only need to know each other
to be reconciled.

Like Cranford, North and South is concerned with the
reconciliation of warring sections of society, but the war
here is more open. Gaskell is returning to the Mary
Barton theme of industrial relations in the manufacturing districts, hoping to make it clearer this time

that her aim was to unite, not antagonise classes. Many
of her friends, middle-class Mancunians as they were,
thought she had given too much of the workers' and
too little of the employers' case in her first novel. She
wrote defensively to Lady Kay-Shuttleworth that she
knew she had represented only one side of the
question, the side she felt most strongly on, and that
she would welcome a treatment of the well-meaning
millowner as hero, but did not have the detailed
knowledge of manufacturing to be able to suggest
specific employment reforms. Citing the experience of
Samuel Greg, a benevolent employer whose schemes
had caused him financial difficulties, she concluded
that

> he, or such as he, might almost be made the hero of a
> fiction on the other side of the question [–] the trials
> of the conscientious rich man, in his dealings with
> the poor. And I should like some *man*, who had a
> man's correct knowledge, to write on this subject.
>
> (*L* 120)

This was in 1850: by 1854, when she was writing *North
and South*, *Cranford* and *Ruth* had given her more
confidence in what a woman's knowledge could bring
to a novel. John Thornton can be seen as her eventual
version of the conscientious rich man, though he is no
philanthropist, but a political economist who is slowly
convinced that if he is to minimise industrial strife he
needs a fuller, more human relationship with his
employees. The 'man's correct knowledge' of the
factory system no longer seems necessary in order to
present this crucial development. The heroine,
Margaret Hale, is Gaskell's agent of reconciliation: she
has a middle-class and a womanly knowledge that,
granted the power to act in the 'man's world', can

transform it. The 'woman's sphere' in *North and South* is apparently restrictive but in fact encompasses more than the man's. As Margaret and her father get to know Milton-Northern, Gaskell makes it clear that they get to know different cities, and the daughter's is closer to the true one:

> After a quiet life in a country parsonage for more than twenty years, there was something dazzling to Mr Hale in the energy which conquered immense difficulties with ease; the power of the machinery of Milton, the power of the men of Milton, impressed him with a sense of grandeur, which he yielded to without caring to inquire into the details of its exercise. But Margaret went less abroad, among machinery and men; saw less of power in its public effect, and, as it happened, she was thrown with one or two of those who, in all measures affecting masses of people, must be acute sufferers for the good of many. The question always is, has everything been done to make the suffering of these exceptions as small as possible? Or, in the triumph of the crowded procession, have the helpless been trampled on, instead of being gently lifted aside out of the roadway of the conqueror, whom they have no power to accompany on his march? (*NS* 108)

Margaret's more domestic life and her household responsibilities, far from restricting her, mean that she comes into contact with the working class. Instead of being dazzled by the power of new technology she enquires into its social implications.

The form of Margaret's and the narrator's question (they are hard to distinguish at this point) already limits the scope of the answer. Suffering is accepted as an inevitable part of industrialisation, and it is seen as the suffering of a few exceptions for the good of everyone else – not the exploitation of all workers for the good of a few millowners. As she befriends the Higgins family and through them the Bouchers, the middle-class heroine learns about the sufferings of the working class. Bessy, wasting away from a disease caused by inhaling fluff from the carding-rooms where she worked, is a dying example of the iniquities of a profit-driven industrial system. The Bouchers struggle to raise a family on poor wages, which local manufacturers want to reduce even further to make their business more competitive in a recession. Nicholas Higgins, the high-minded trades unionist who advocates and takes part in strike action, has the best of all Gaskellian reasons for it: he is acting for the good of others. Yet, despite this and despite the riot scene that depicts the strength of the workers' desperation, the concentration on a few individuals reinforces the narrative suggestion that the casualties of industrial capitalism are exceptions to the rule. In *Mary Barton*, where more working-class families are depicted, their sufferings seem representative of a whole class that is placed, radically, at the centre of the action. Here, with the return to a middle-class centre of consciousness, Gaskell makes working-class suffering seem more simply personal and more manageable.

The heroine's role in *North and South* is a weightier one than in any other Gaskell novel. Margaret is not always the centre of consciousness: the narrative enters the consciousness of other characters, especially John Thornton, Mrs Thornton, Mr Hale; very seldom, significantly, Nicholas Higgins. The heroine is, though, the narrative's most persistent focus. The story of Margaret's maturing and coming to terms with the new society represented by the North is combined with the story of that society's coming to terms with itself and glimpsing the possibility of better social relations. Margaret is a crucial agent here. She is Gaskell's most Ruskinian woman, performing a vital social work that is an extension of her personal duties. At the beginning of the novel she thinks of herself as going to take up 'the important post of only daughter in Helstone parsonage' (36). Gaskell is at one with her heroine in this estimate of the significance of the daughter's role in a genteel home: Margaret will combine dedication to her parents' welfare with a 'lady bountiful' role among the rural poor. After the move to Milton she finds her role changing: no longer the vicar's daughter but the daughter of an obscure tutor, she has no status in the northern city's public life. Soon, though, her friendships give her an important role in the community, as she argues about industrial relations with both the millowner Thornton and the worker Higgins. Higgins forces her to change her attitude to the poor, scorning as impertinence her automatic attempt to become a charitable lady-visitor in his home; but he accepts her friendship when offered as from an equal. Margaret becomes a mediator between classes, representing the views of each to the other, arguing for connection and the explanation of differences. This role supersedes, but also grows out of, that of the daughter in Helstone Parsonage. Only a woman, and a woman of the middle class, could do what Margaret does in Milton. Her job is nothing less than to transform the harsh world of Victorian *laissez-faire* capitalism, by taking the values of home out into the world.

In her arguments with Thornton she opposes his rigidly segmented view of the relations between employer and employees (he should dictate their actions during working hours and ignore them outside those hours) with an insistence on the bond that religious duties tie between all people. As in *Mary*

Barton, there is no attempt to argue against the employers' policy on wages, only a demand that it be properly explained to the workers. When the strike threatens to become violent, with strikers converging on Thornton's mill, where he has introduced 'knobstick' (blackleg) labour, Margaret intervenes dramatically to promote dialogue instead of violence. She insists that Thornton go to speak to the men rather than let troops break up the demonstration, and then goes to protect him from the crowd's violence. She is injured by a stone intended for Thornton, and at the sight of her blood the men are subdued, and disperse. This scene can be read as the mythical confrontation between the passionate, animal nature of the working class and the civilising influence of middle-class womanliness: Margaret, through being the victim of an attack with sexual overtones, gains a 'womanly' power to satiate passion and contain violence.[5]

Thornton and his family personalise Margaret's gesture, reading it as a declaration of love for him, whereas she sees her intervention as part of a general womanly calling, loftily explaining to Thornton, 'we all feel the sanctity of our sex as a high privilege when we see danger' (252) and 'any woman, worthy of the name of woman, would come forward to shield, with her reverenced helplessness, a man in danger' (253). Femininity has become a religious vocation. The heroine is surely protesting too much: events have already shown that 'if she thought her sex would be a protection . . . she was wrong' (234); and she is clearly more sexually attracted to Thornton than she can admit to herself. Under pressure from idealistic conventions of femininity, she divorces her public role from her private feelings, seeing herself as an icon of femininity rather than an individual woman. As she sees it either her action is purely impersonal, for the public good, or privately, sexually motivated and shameful. She cannot accept that she is both attracted to Thornton and genuinely concerned for the welfare of everyone in the crowd. Margaret's difficulty here brings into focus Gaskell's problem of trying to create a heroic woman within the ideological constraints of sexually pure Victorian femininity. Margaret is continually surrounded by what P. N. Furbank has called 'a curious and special "heroine" style': references to her stateliness and dignity abound, and seem to cry out for some ironic distancing on the author's part, yet they are not clearly placed as part of the heroine's self-image, but seem to come simply from the narrator.[5] Furbank criticises Gaskell's 'collusion' with a self-deceiving heroine who keeps giving straight fearless looks as she tells lies, but Gaskell is well aware of Margaret's failure to live up to the heroic ideal. After she lies to protect her brother Frederick, Margaret realises that her early aspiration to be 'sans peur et sans reproche', a feminine version of a chivalric knight-at-arms, is unrealisable (502); but the heroic attempt is no subject for Gaskell's irony. She admires Margaret for trying and for recognising failure. She does show how Margaret's motives are inevitably misunderstood in a world that only sees *man's* honour as truthfulness, woman's being chastity. While Margaret torments herself because Thornton knows she has told a lie, he is only concerned because he thinks she was out walking with a lover: once he knows the man was her brother he does not care how much she lied, the important thing is that she has not been 'unmaidenly' (515).

Margaret's dramatic public intervention at the riot-scene averts immediate violence, but does not solve any problems in the long term. The strike ends with the workers defeated and bitter. Margaret's next important intervention is more private, less direct and less liable to misinterpretation in sexual terms. She persuades Nicholas Higgins, now blacklisted by employers for his union activities, to ask Thornton for work. He reluctantly agrees, saying that this is the 'first time in my life as e'er I give way to a woman' (383). Margaret retorts: 'I don't believe you: I believe you have just given way to wife and daughters as much as most men' (384). She is right: Higgins has already shown the influence of 'womanly' values by his care of the Boucher children. Her influence is only to make him realise that to put these values into practice he must come to some reconciliation with the employers. When Thornton refuses Higgins's request, with a bitter reference to woman's meddling, it is an attempted repudiation of womanly influence arising from his estrangement from Margaret; but later, his own feelings of sympathy with a man who waited five hours to speak to him, combined with a sense of justice, make him investigate Higgins's circumstances, and when he finds the story about Boucher's children to be true he offers work after all. An uneasy truce develops between the two men, which leads to neighbourly connections (Thornton takes an interest in the Boucher children and helps with their schooling) and to a few tentative reforms at the mill, such as the workers' canteen. Thornton, like Margaret before him, is anxious not to have his behaviour construed in terms of sexual attraction, and like her he is more influenced by it than he admits. But it is not simply a case of sexual love softening a stern man's heart. Margaret's influence has helped to call out a 'womanly' compassion always latent in him, and has persuaded him that this side of his character can be given some public expression.

Thus Margaret acts most successfully by bringing out the womanliness within men. Her and Gaskell's message is that womanly values should be adopted in the public world that men control, and by men themselves. When she embodies this message publicly and directly, the contradictions between her interpretation of a woman's role and society's definitions of sexual propriety are made painfully visible. She can only reconcile the two by channelling woman's influence in more private ways. In the denouement she agrees to marry Thornton, and her money will go to rebuilding his business along new lines influenced by her earlier arguments and example. Like other Victorian heroines, she exchanges economic power and an independent position for a spiritual and moral authority.[7]

The idea of a woman compensating for the lack of economic and political power with a position of moral authority offering public influence is one that women writers of the nineteenth century might apply to themselves as well as their heroines. The influence attributed to the novel by Victorian commentators is, after all, close to their notion of woman's influence. The Victorian novel is generally about domestic life, centrally concerned with romantic love and marriage, and yet can comment on the world outside. It praises 'womanly' values of love and compassion, and is written for the middle-class fireside where women's influence is supposed to reign. So by writing, in works as diverse as *Cranford* and *North and South*, fables of reconciliation between classes and sexes through the operation of womanly values, Gaskell was exercising a peculiarly Victorian mode of womanly authority. Like Margaret Hale she was bringing a 'womanly' influence to bear on the public scene by working on people's private emotions.

5 History and Tyranny: *Sylvia's Lovers*

Gaskell's novels of contemporary or near-contemporary life are committed to an optimistic assessment of how an individual's actions can affect social developments. *North and South* especially, as we have seen, assigns a crucial importance to the heroine's role as mediator in the class war. In *Sylvia's Lovers* she adopts the more pessimistic view of human agency typical of the nineteenth-century historical novel pioneered by Scott, whose heroes are typically caught up in large historical events on which they can have little or no impact. Gaskell had always been fascinated by history, and during the 1850s had written stories based on historical events, including 'Lois the Witch' (1858) about the Salem witch trials, and 'My Lady Ludlow' with its inset narrative about victims of the guillotine during the French Revolution. With *Sylvia's Lovers* she turned to the full-length historical novel, and like other novelists at the same time – George Eliot in *Adam Bede*, Dickens in *A Tale of Two Cities* – she turned to the events of the 1790s. Like George Eliot, she is concerned not with the events that make up official history, the actions of kings and generals – but the everyday life of ordinary people trapped in a particular environment at a particular era: the story of the powerless. Unlike the George Eliot of *Adam Bede*, though, she emphasises throughout how fundamentally the obscure lives of her characters are determined by political decisions they know practically nothing about. Gaskell presents the England of the 1790s as in the grip of a despotic government that has passed an 'oppressive act against seditious meetings' in a bid to wipe out support for radical politics (*SL* 167). The law is obedient to government policy instead of to justice, and people like the shopkeepers John and Jeremiah Foster, who as Dissenters are probably on the side of those few pioneers arguing for Parliamentary reform, have to be very careful how they talk about politics (*SL* 168). The novel's dramatic embodiment of government tyranny is the press-gang.

The press-gang's activities dominate *Sylvia's Lovers*. The Admiralty's impressment during the war with France is described in the first chapter, and the crucial determining actions of the narrative turn on its operations. The press-gang's attack on a returning whaler, which leads to Darley's death and Kinraid's wounding; Kinraid's own impressment; the freeing of the impressed prisoners, and the burning of the Randyvowse, which leads to Daniel Robson's execution – these events are all based on historical records of similar incidents on the north-eastern coast of England in the 1790s.[1] They are tied together in the narrative by their significance in Sylvia Robson's life. The early description of the attack on the whaling-ship establishes her closeness in feeling to the outraged Monkshaven community. The wounded Kinraid first attracts her as a local hero; with his impressment she loses her lover, with Daniel's execution she loses her father. Affected to an unusual degree by measures that affect all in her community, and exceptionally noticeable because of her beauty and liveliness, her importance as a heroine is that she is a particularly vivid representative of Monkshaven life. Being 'of that impressible nature that takes the tone of feeling from those surrounding' (18), she can be made to typify Monkshaven community feeling: mutually supportive, passionate and violent in defence of its own. Her fate is a particularly intense version of all Monkshaven people's: helpless against government power and unable to gain more than a glimpse of understanding of the historical and political forces shaping their lives.

Gaskell interweaves Sylvia's individual story with that of the Monkshaven community. The first few chapters mingle her trip to the market and to Foster's clothing shop, her friendship with Molly Corney and her relations with her cousin Philip Hepburn, with the drama of the press-gang's attack on the returning whaling-ship. As these two narrative strands emerge there are indications of how closely Sylvia's individual emotional history is to mirror the general fate of Monkshaven people. Sylvia and Molly Corney enter the town at a time of mounting excitement as the first whaling ship of the season is expected in harbour, and while Sylvia is in Foster's shop buying her cloak, the press-gang arrest some of the returning sailors. The focus is on women waiting for their menfolk and suddenly robbed of them. As the press-gang, surrounded by a hostile crowd, pushes through the town with its captives, men's voices are drowned by a preponderance of

> women crying aloud, throwing up their arms in imprecation, showering down abuse as hearty and rapid as if they had been a Greek chorus. Their wild, famished eyes were strained on faces they might not kiss, their cheeks were flushed to purple with anger or else livid with impotent craving for revenge. (29)

Sylvia, sympathising with their emotions as a few minutes earlier she had shared their delight, pushes to the door of the shop longing to help. Her later relationship with the shopman Philip is prefigured in his reaction to her behaviour here: scolding her for shaking hands with 'Newcastle Bess', one of 'the lowest class of seaport inhabitants' (27), and trying to keep her indoors with the argument that 'it's the law, and no one can do aught against it, least of all women and lasses' (28), he represents the masculine upholder of law trying to control unruly feminine behaviour by keeping 'his' woman separate and secluded. The interlocking of Sylvia's emotional state with the public event is made complete at the climax of this scene. The focus is on what the watchers outside Foster's shop witness, and it narrows from the crowd of angry women to the cry of one particular woman, who comes rushing from the bridge after being told,

> by a score of busy, sympathising voices, that her husband was kidnapped for the service of the Government.
> She had need pause in the market-place, the outlet of which was crammed up. Then she gave tongue for the first time in such a fearful shriek, you could hardly catch the words she said.
> 'Jamie! Jamie! will they not let you to me?'
> Those were the last words Sylvia heard before her own hysterical burst of tears called everyone's attention to her. (29–30)

Sylvia's outburst expresses the emotional turmoil of all the women in the crowd, helping establish her as the representative voice of Monkshaven womanhood, while Jamie's wife's loss prefigures Sylvia's own loss of a lover when Kinraid is captured.

Public and private oppressions combine to make Kinraid's capture tragic to Sylvia. The press-gang, operating illegally in imprisoning a protected whaler (216), are the instruments of an oppressive government. Philip, who, witnessing the capture but failing to report it, is responsible for Sylvia's belief in Kinraid's death, acts from a possessive love that is equally oppressive in its manifestations. Again, while her parents' tragedies – her father's execution and her mother's subsequent witlessness – are the result of government policy, it is Philip who compounds these disasters for Sylvia by the way he 'rescues' her. Believing her lover dead and wanting only to provide her mother with a home, Sylvia marries Philip, and the once-lively young woman becomes a listless wife in the parlour behind the shop. For all Philip's outward gentleness and his genuine concern for her and her family, he press-gangs Sylvia into marriage.

Even to make the division between public and private tyranny may be to distort Gaskell's vision here. All kinds of social institutions – the military, the law and marriage – are criticised. Gaskell makes her clearest attack on forms of institutionalised authority, whether of admirals, judges or husbands. The rescue of the press-gang's victims from the Randyvowse, led by Daniel Robson, is presented as wholly admirable in itself, but taken too far when the men go on to burn down the inn. Sylvia's implacable hatred of the man who betrayed her father, and her later vow to repudiate her marriage, are her version of this violent spirit, and her behaviour is equally seen as an understandable reaction, taken too far. The emphasis throughout is on the immense provocations that all these rebels have had. Gone is the paltering of *Mary Barton*, where the narrative voice anxiously denies the political implications of what it documents. The actions of the Admiralty are roundly called 'tyranny' (6). Defence of government action comes in reported speech, clearly distanced from the narrative voice:

Government took up the attack on the Rendezvous

with a high and heavy hand. It was necessary to assert authority which had been of late too often braved. An example must be made, to strike dismay into those who opposed and defied the press-gang; and all the minor authorities who held their powers from Government were in a similar manner severe and relentless in the execution of their duty. So the attorney, who went over to see the prisoner in York Castle, told Philip. (307)

The writer who, in *Mary Barton* and *North and South*, seemed only hesitantly in favour of the rights of workers to form unions and to strike, and who unequivocally condemned any violence on their part, comes in *Sylvia's Lovers* to support resistance to the government and to accept the rebels' violence as regrettable but inevitable. The novelist whose writing became tangled as she acknowledged the existence of female sexual desire in *Ruth*, here casually allows Sylvia, married to Philip, to betray how much she longs for another man: this is no source of shame for Sylvia or embarrassment for her creator. The much more radical questioning of conventions and institutions in *Sylvia's Lovers* belies the claim that Gaskell had turned to 'non-political' writing.[2]

What she had done, though, was to turn away from the topical issues of capitalist industrial relations and unmarried motherhood, which drew attention to the political project of her earlier novels, to less obviously immediate social questions and a historical narrative form that would not be interpreted as political. Adopting the historian's perspective freed her to criticise the values of her class and time by moving the contest onto safer ground. She ensured both that she could express more rebellion and that she would not be read as rebellious.

Daniel and Sylvia Robson, in their different ways the two most rebellious characters, are made safe by historical distance. They are presented as almost primitive people whose rebelliousness is an aspect of their childlike simplicity. Crucial to the presentation of the Robsons and of the Monkshaven people generally is the notion that the typical human consciousness has changed greatly in the sixty years separating the world recorded in *Sylvia's Lovers* from the time of its composition:

> It is astonishing to look back and find how differ- ently constituted were the minds of most people fifty or sixty years ago; they felt, they understood, without going through reasoning or analytic pro- cesses, and if this was the case among the more educated people, of course it was still more so in the class to which Sylvia belonged. (318)

The unreasoning intuitiveness of Monkshaven people serves a double purpose for the historical narrative: allowing the historian to elevate the primitive and criticise the over-sophisticated modern mind, but also providing a check on the more radical political implica- tions of the narrative. The rebellious actions of Daniel Robson are also the actions of a man 'very like a child in all the parts of his character . . . [who] acted on im- pulse, and too often had reason to be sorry for it' (247).

Gaskell's attitude to the simplicity of her charac- ters is ambivalent. With reference to Sylvia's ready acceptance of Hester Rose's greater goodness, the narrator comments on the unreflective mind of the late eighteenth century:

> In the agricultural counties, and among the class to which these four people belonged, [Sylvia, Molly,

Hester and Philip: farmers and shopkeepers] there is little analysis of motive or comparison of characters and actions, even at this present day of enlightenment. Sixty or seventy years ago there was still less. I do not mean that amongst thoughtful and serious people there was not much reading of such books as *Mason on Self-Knowledge*, and *Law's Serious Call*, or that there were not the experiences of the Wesleyans, that were related at class-meeting for the edification of the hearers. But, taken for a general rule, it may be said that few knew what manner of men they were, compared to the numbers now who are fully conscious of their virtues, qualities, failings, and weaknesses, and who go about comparing others with themselves – not in a spirit of Pharisaism and arrogance, but with a vivid self-consciousness that more than anything else deprives characters of freshness and originality.

To return to the party we left standing on the high-raised footway that ran along the bridle-road to Haytersbank. Sylvia had leisure in her heart to think 'how good Hester is for sitting with the poor bed-ridden sister of Darley!' without having a pang of self-depreciation in the comparison of her own conduct with that which she was capable of so fully appreciating. She had gone to church for the ends of vanity, and remained to the funeral for curiosity and the pleasure of the excitement. In this way a modern young lady would have condemned herself, and therefore lost the simple, purifying pleasure of admiration of another. (74–5)

The narrator clearly approves of Sylvia's lack of introspection. A heroine's inability to make moral comparisons, her unawareness of her own shortcomings, would be exactly the right material for ironic mockery

of her in an Austen novel: Emma, particularly, is
frequently laughed at for just this gap between her
appreciation of what is right and her blindness to her
own faults. Gaskell's irony is elsewhere. The moralising
comment on Sylvia's behaviour in going to church 'for
the ends of vanity' seems on first encounter to come
from the narrator, but the following sentence places it
instead as the hypothetical comment of a conscience-
stricken 'modern young lady', perhaps a representative
of Gaskell's imagined readers, who is the real ironic
target. Self-knowledge, that moral desideratum of the
Austenian novel, is here seen as inadequate, even
dangerous, because of its link with self-absorption.

This narrative view chimes with views Gaskell
expressed elsewhere about self-consciousness, in
relation both to personal life and to writing. 'I
believe . . . that we ought not to be too cognizant of our
mental proceedings, only taking note of the results', she
advised Herbert Grey, author of the novel *The Three
Paths*, in 1859: 'But certainly – whether introspection be
morbid or not, – it is not a safe training for a novelist. It
is a weakening of the art which has crept in of late
years' (*L* 541).[3] In *Sylvia's Lovers* the characteristic
minds of Sylvia's time and place are presented as
nearer to purity, able to take pleasure, having everything that the morbid modern consciousness has lost.
Romanticising the past for its noble simplicity, the
narrator is nevertheless not condemning the present.
The self-conscious moderns sincerely pursue the good,
they are not Pharasaical or arrogant; what they lack is
the 'freshness and originality' she finds in more
primitive minds. The Monkshaven characters exem-
plify for her both the 'poetry of humble life' and of the
past. Gaskell's view of history here echoes Macaulay's:
'as civilization advances, poetry almost necessarily
declines'.[4] Characters like Sylvia become poetic objects

for the novelist, helping her to avoid the modern danger, spelled out in the letter to Herbert Grey, of forsaking external for internal reality. Like the 'healthy' writer Defoe, Gaskell 'sets *objects* not *feelings*' before the reader (*L* 541).

Yet the self-consciousness that deprives characters of freshness is itself described as 'vivid', suggesting that what modern characters lose in the outward charms of primitive simplicity, they might gain in intensity. Certainly *Sylvia's Lovers* is not without 'modern' concentration on feelings, as we can see if we compare some of the 'simple' characters in it with Philip Hepburn. Although the passage quoted above seems to class him with the unreflecting farmers and shop-keepers of sixty years ago, Philip of all the characters in the novel is an example of 'vivid self-consciousness'; in his tendency to gloomy self-examination he is the most 'modern' mind in Monkshaven. This does him no good morally – quite the reverse – but it makes him interesting to his creator despite her mistrust of introspection, and in the end it enables him to carry the burden of her conception of tragic experience better than her more 'primitive' characters.

The narrative is often focused on Philip's inner life: his jealous obsession with Sylvia, and the moral dilemmas to which it gives rise. Gaskell does not concentrate exclusively on his experience, but according to her usual practice, frequently shifts point of view within the narrative, and alternates between internal and external presentations of character. Not only Philip Hepburn and Sylvia Robson but Charley Kinraid, Daniel and Bell Robson, Alice and Hester Rose, and others, have their turn as centre of consciousness for some part of the narrative. In the scenes where Philip is present, though, there is a noticeable tendency to concentrate on his thoughts, imagination and feelings.

In 'New Year's Fête' (chapter 12), for example, we learn of Bell Robson's illness, Sylvia's care of her, and the New Year party at the Corneys', where Sylvia's relationship with Charley Kinraid begins to blossom. The part of protagonist in this chapter fluctuates between Sylvia, from whose point of view much of the party is described, and Philip, with occasional glimpses into the minds of Charley Kinraid, Bell Robson and others. The chapter opens and closes on Philip as the narrative centre, and his feelings are minutely unfolded during its course. The narrative voice approaches him as a historically distant figure to be recorded from the outside, whose concerns are suffused with the pathos belonging to all things past:

> At this hour, all the actors in this story having played out their parts and gone to their rest, there is something touching in recording the futile efforts made by Philip to win from Sylvia the love he yearned for.

The vantage point then shifts from the narrator's present to a closer concern with the time of the narrative, still treating Philip externally. He becomes a mildly comic figure:

> But, at the time, any one who had watched him might have been amused to see the grave, awkward, plain young man studying patterns and colours for a new waistcoat, with his head a little on one side. (133)

Within a paragraph this style of presentation has been modulated as the narrative voice moves closer to Philip's consciousness, until it is recording his mental exclamations:

This ribbon was quite a different kind of present; he touched it tenderly, as if he were caressing it, when he thought of her wearing it; the briar-rose (sweetness and thorns) seemed to be the very flower for her; the soft, green ground on which the pink and brown pattern ran, was just the colour to show off her complexion. And she would in a way belong to him: her cousin, her mentor, her chaperon, her lover! While others only admired, he might hope to appropriate; for of late they had been such happy friends! (134)

When Kinraid and Sylvia meet, the narrative presents their thoughts, paying close attention to Sylvia's, and rather less to Kinraid's; but closest attention of all is given to Philip, the jealous observer. Sylvia is a picture he is watching:

More playing with her apron-string, and head hung still lower down, though the corners of her mouth would go up in a shy smile of pleasure. Philip watched it all as greedily as if it gave him delight. (142)

Philip's voyeurism, his anxious mental activity and his insistent questioning of the meaning of what he sees – 'Why did they linger near each other? Why did Sylvia look so dreamily happy . . . ?' (149) – contrasts with Kinraid's active participation in the party, his untroubled mind and his confidence in his ability to interpret the world around him:

After the Robsons had left, a blank fell upon both Charley and Philip. In a few minutes, however, the former, accustomed to prompt decision, resolved that she and no other should be his wife. Accustomed to

> popularity among women, and well versed in the
> incipient signs of their liking for him, he anticipated
> no difficulty in winning her. Satisfied with the past,
> and pleasantly hopeful about the future, he found it
> easy to turn his attention to the next prettiest girl in
> the room. (153)

Kinraid's behaviour here foreshadows his later ability
to replace his lost Sylvia with another love, and typifies
an attitude to past and future that allows him to adapt
to his environment and absorb historical change. This
specksioneer, representative of a picturesque way of life
that belongs to the past, seems a quintessential victim
of historical forces when he is taken by the press-gang
and forced into the English–French wars; but he
eventually becomes a captain and raises his social
status through marriage. The 'primitive' preference for
acting over thinking, the lack of self-questioning, which
Gaskell sees as typical of the rural lower classes and of
the past, are also the traits that make for success in the
world and adaptation to the future. Charley Kinraid
will live on into a new generation, while Philip
Hepburn will die young.

We are rarely brought closer to Charley's consciousness than in the passage cited above: his thoughts are
simple, easily summarised, and of little interest to the
narrator. The contrast with Philip is evident in the
following paragraph, which turns from Kinraid's
'ready good temper and buoyant spirit' to the 'wet
blanket' Philip, with an immediate increase in intensity
of feeling: 'The cold sleet almost blinded him as the
sea-wind drove it straight in his face; it cut against him
as it was blown with drifting force' (153). This is perhaps just to say that Philip Hepburn is Gaskell's tragic
hero, while Charley Kinraid is a colourful background
figure. The change from 'The Specksioneer' to 'Philip's

Idol' as working titles for the novel suggest Gaskell's
shift of interest from Charley to Philip, and from the
past as picturesque to psychological drama.

The decision to focus more on Philip reveals
something of Gaskell's views of the relation between
history and character. Philip is the novel's thinker, for
all the limitations Gaskell places upon his cast of
thought. He is introspective and self-examining, and
though not sophisticated in his outlook and usually
mistaken in his judgement, he shares the narrator's
own stance as observer and her ability to analyse
events. He even has his own tentative theory of history.
When he hears from Jeremiah Foster about Alice Rose's
rejection of a quiet man of business and her unhappy
marriage to a sailor in a whaling-ship, he draws
parallels with his own and Charley's rivalry over
Sylvia:

> Philip fell to thinking; a generation ago something of
> the same kind had been going on as that which he
> was now living through, quick with hopes and fears.
> A girl beloved by two – nay, those two so identical in
> occupation as he and Kinraid were – Rose identi-
> cal even in character with what he knew of the
> specksioneer; a girl choosing the wrong lover, and
> suffering and soured all her life in consequence of
> her youth's mistake; was that to be Sylvia's lot? – or,
> rather, was she not saved from it by the event of the
> impressment, and by the course of silence he himself
> had resolved upon? Then he went on to wonder if
> the lives of one generation were but a repetition of
> the lives of those who had gone before, with no
> variation but from the internal cause that some had
> greater capacity for suffering than others. Would
> those very circumstances which made the interest of

his life now, return, in due cycle, when he was dead and Sylvia was forgotten?

Perplexed thoughts of this and a similar kind kept returning into Philip's mind whenever he had leisure to give himself up to consideration of anything but the immediate throng of business. And every time he dwelt on this complication and succession of similar events, he emerged from his reverie more and more satisfied with the course he had taken in withholding from Sylvia all knowledge of her lover's fate. (240)

Other characters in the novel construct histories by telling the story of their own lives or by interpreting other people's stories. Thus in William Coulson's version of history, his sister died mainly because of her disappointed love for Charley Kinraid, who 'kept company' with her for two years and then left her (192) – an event that does not seem to be part of Kinraid's own complacent view of his past. Daniel Robson, like Philip, evidently trusts history to repeat itself. Kinraid's courtship of Sylvia reminds him of his courtship of Bell, and his approval of Kinraid as a suitor is based on what the two men have in common: both have been specksioneers in whaling-ships, both have defied the law, and both can win women's interest with their tall tales of adventurous life in the man's world of the seas. While these characters make up kinds of history, they formulate no ideas about it. Philip, on the other hand, is capable of generalising from his experience and trying out the notion of a cyclic view of history. As he does so the Yorkshire dialect of his direct speeches gives way to a modern, standard language use, suggesting a momentary collapsing of the distance between narrator and character. It is as if Philip is now sharing the role of the historian.

There remains a distinction, though, between the

narrator's attitude to events and Philip Hepburn's. She does not share his cyclic view of history; rather, she reveals how the various characters, from their different points of view, perceive different parallels between past and present. Philip takes Alice Rose's disastrous marriage to a whaler who 'went after other women, and drank, and beat her' (240) as a prediction of Sylvia's likely fate if she marries Kinraid; Daniel Robson, without consciously considering the matter, takes his own, in his view satisfactory, marriage as a good omen for his daughter's marriage to another sailor. Yet what the narrative has revealed of Kinraid's character does not warrant the assumption that he would behave like Jack Rose, while the indications of some of Bell Robson's difficulties with married life, and her evident wish that her daughter not marry a similar kind of man, belie her husband's optimistic view of Sylvia and Kinraid's relationship. The historical parallels Philip notices have no predictive force: no determinist, even in her use of a form that lends itself to determinism, Gaskell places moral responsibility firmly on the individual's reaction to historical predicament. Philip notices the parallel between Jack Rose and Charley Kinraid, but does not understand the parallel between his own position, as rejected lover, and John Foster's. Foster has reacted to rejection by quietly offering Alice Rose financial help, and by planning to leave all his money to her daughter – a complete contrast to Philip's selfish pursuit of Sylvia. The novel's view of history is that it is a series of stories that it is up to the individual to interpret: viewed as simple reflections of the individual's own preoccupations they merely help compound existing errors, but viewed as moral exempla they might help him or her to act well.

Philip, with his oppressive pursuit of Sylvia, and the cruel deception that he so carefully rationalises, is the most culpable character in the novel, the one least the victim of external forces. Yet this is what makes him interesting to Gaskell, and makes her focus on him as tragic hero rather than on Daniel Robson, the rebellious but doomed victim of government injustice. In the end she is less interested in exploring the historical conflict between governors and governed than in the internal conflicts of characters seen as relatively free moral agents. Daniel Robson's fate illustrates the helplessness of an ordinary man caught up in historical events beyond his control; Philip's does not, though he becomes a soldier and returns from the wars a broken man. He chooses to enlist out of shame when Kinraid returns and Sylvia rejects her husband, and by saving Kinraid's life on the battlefield he atones for his earlier action. History, as exemplified in the siege of Acre, has become mere background for the working-out of an individual's moral salvation. Gaskell's treatment of the siege of Acre has been criticised as a melodramatic lapse in a realistic historical novel, but it is necessary to understand its function: the rehabilitation of a form of heroism even as conventional battle-heroics are mocked. The soldiers understand little of the causes of the war and Kinraid's courage goes along with a childish naïvety:[5] real heroism is not in battle but in Philip's rescue of the man he had wronged and hated.

As J. M. Rignall has pointed out, Sylvia's two lovers swop roles during the novel: Kinraid from being the representative of an old heroic way of life changes to become a social success in the new century; Philip, the unheroic, new bourgeois man, becomes a heroic rescuer and a social outcast. The changes are entirely consistent with the two men's characters: Kinraid's opportunism, Philip's obsessive commitment.[6] Thus the novel resists any schematic linking of characters' social position and occupation to the historical narrative of the decline of

old ways of life and the development of nineteenth-
century society. Character is strongly influenced but not
completely determined by social, regional and historical position; individual temperament is given a great
deal of weight too. At the end of the novel the
historical narrative recedes and there is a brief picture
of Monkshaven as it is in the narrator's own time, no
longer a whaling community but a Victorian seaside
resort. Kinraid, the former whaler, would be more at
home there than Philip.

Philip's character, then, is shifting in its relation to
historical development. In the earlier part of the novel
when his inner life is the focus of much attention he
exemplifies the perplexities of the more modern,
introspective cast of mind; outwardly a man perfectly
fitted to his station, a spokesman for conformity, but
inwardly alienated from his surroundings, watching
life secretly and anxiously. By the end of the novel he
has metamorphosed into something clearer and
simpler – a penitent whose guilt can be externally
expressed in the confession to Sylvia that 'I ha' made
thee my idol' (495), and whose alienation from the
social world receives appropriate external expression in
his reappearance at Monkshaven as a hermit and a
beggar. He does what he can to atone for his sin by the
rescue of Kinraid, and finally by the rescue of Bella, his
and Sylvia's daughter, from drowning. The rescue at
Acre is told in a deliberately 'dreamlike' way, 'like an
attempt in another world to redeem the errors of this',[7]
and from this time on Philip clearly belongs to and is
headed for another world. It is as if Philip's modern,
brooding mind leads to errors that can only be atoned
for by simple, unreflecting heroic action – action that
takes away Philip's identity as representative of a new
kind of man and returns him to an innocent past.

Philip's reconciliation with Sylvia comes about only

as he is dying, from injuries received during the rescue of Bella. Sylvia, now 'a sad, pale woman, allays dressed in black' (502), dies herself before Bella is grown. Like Philip, she has become a tragic figure. Her refusal to forgive Philip, her vow never to live with him as his wife again are 'sorely punished' (496) by the reconciliation that comes too late.

Sylvia is less the centre of narrative attention than Gaskell's heroines usually are. Her background and daily life are created in sympathetic detail, and she is presented as loving and generous, capable of great feeling and suffering but not of complex thought. Her mind is not interesting to her creator in the way that Margaret Hale's is. As the representative of the unreflecting character belonging to the past, she does not, at least in the early part of the novel, receive the attention to her inner life that is accorded Philip. The unembarrassed ease with which Gaskell can portray this heroine's sexuality is a function of Sylvia's lack of troubling consciousness: her vitality and sexuality can be simply and vividly conveyed through the symbolic red cloak. Later in the narrative, when unhappiness has made her more thoughtful, this is again easily summed up in externals – the mourning clothes she inappropriately wears to her wedding, the black dresses of her widowhood. It is not the development of a thoughtful heroine so much as the loss of a lively one.

Gaskell's picture of historical development in this novel is a sombre one. The vital, heroic, rebellious past, so vividly evoked in the early chapters, is progressively distanced till, in the final paragraphs, it has become a not very reliable local legend. Those who embody its values – Sylvia and, in the end, Philip – have tragic fates, while those who will go on to succeed in the new century, like Kinraid, do so by losing their heroic glamour and becoming merely ordinary. Adaptation and survival, so roundly celebrated in *North and South*, are tinged here with melancholy and loss. The forced religious conclusion attempts to cancel out the complexities of history and consciousness by a return to moral absolutes: sin, repentance, forgiveness and a vision of heaven provide a framework giving meaning to tragic experience. But the relativity encouraged by the historical narrative lingers. Early in the novel, characters' thoughts and moral standards have been shown as at least partly the product of historical circumstance; and their own views of the past as fictions shaped by desire. At its end 'popular feeling, and ignorance of the real facts', have changed Philip's and Sylvia's experience into a story of a man who 'died of starvation while his wife lived in hard-hearted plenty' (502). We have to look, in the words of the novel's epigraph from Tennyson, 'behind the veil' to find the truth of forgiveness and reconciliation. Yet the narrative's own revelations of how history is distorted in the telling make it more difficult for the reader to pay the tribute of implicit trust demanded by the traditional omniscient narrator. How does she have access to a truth beyond the popular legends? Her interpretation of the narrative is shaped by desire too – the urgent desire for a religious meaning that will obviate the threat that life may prove, in Tennyson's words again, 'futile' as well as 'frail'.[8]

6 Household Goodness: 'Cousin Phillis', *Wives and Daughters*

Towards the end of her writing career, Gaskell gained a new sense of confidence in her work. 'Cousin Phillis' (1863–4) and *Wives and Daughters*, the enchanting 'everyday story' which she had not quite finished when she died, display a new and dazzling sureness of artistic control. Edgar Wright explains this development in terms of a move from direct authorial commentary to more impersonal narrative methods. In 'Cousin Phillis' the narrator is a major character in the story, and in *Wives and Daughters* the omniscient narrator withdraws to the background, leaving Molly Gibson, in Henry James's terms, the 'fine central intelligence' that gives the novel a unified viewpoint. (As Wright points out, James admired Gaskell's final novel).[1] This artistic development is sometimes assumed to entail a movement away from the social commitment of her earlier fiction. Wright praises her for dropping the 'didactic element' in her later work, and sees 'Cousin Phillis' and *Wives and Daughters* as a return to 'the Cranford world', a place whose values are so much 'part of her own nature' that she does not need to judge it in social, moral or religious terms: 'she needs only to demonstrate'.[2] Thus Gaskell seems to achieve artistic greatness at the expense of social analysis. Yet 'Cousin Phillis' and *Wives and Daughters* contain social commentary all the more telling for being subtly rendered. Patsy Stoneman offers a more helpful approach to Gaskell's later achievements when she argues that in *Wives and Daughters* Gaskell uses the authority of a realist stance to make the 'Woman Question', which had been present, but unfocused, in earlier novels, into a central issue, 'the acknowledged subject of debate'.[3]

Gaskell's late work shows the fruits, not of a movement from anxious social commitment to artistic freedom from commitment, but of a transformed view of the artist, and especially the woman artist. She is no longer fundamentally split into dutiful and escapist halves. That earlier view, articulated in her correspondence with a fellow woman artist in 1850 (see above, pp. 4–6) haunts much of Gaskell's work, but the later Gaskell is able to imagine a healing of the split, so that social commitment and enchantment need not preclude each other.

We can find her considering the possibility of this new synthesis in one of the short stories she wrote for the *Cornhill Magazine* in 1860, 'Curious, If True'. The mode of expression is itself an indication of the later Gaskell's greater confidence: whereas her earlier doubts about the artistic vocation were anxiously expressed in private letters, the later work publicly presented a kind of parable about artistic vocation, delivered in a light, playful manner. Praised for its delicacy of humour, this 'lively *jeu d'esprit*'[4] is worth examining for its dramatisation and visionary healing of the split within the artist.

Subtitled 'Extract from a letter from Richard Whittingham, Esq.', the story consists of this gentleman's narrative of a 'curious' and 'dream-like' experience that happened to him one summer evening in France. The narrator is visiting that country to pursue some

research into his own family history. He is a descendant
of Calvin's sister, and believes that he may find some
distant relatives, also collateral descendants of Calvin.
What he finds instead is a group of strange people who
claim kinship with him on a very different basis. One
evening when he is staying in Tours he takes a walk in
the woods and gets lost. Just as he is resigning himself
to a night in the open he sees a large château in the
distance, and goes to ask for shelter. Identifying himself
as 'Richard Whittingham, an English gentleman', he is
immediately welcomed as a long-expected guest by the
porter, who incidentally is as large as a giant. When the
porter goes on to ask whether he has brought
'Monsieur le Géanquilleur' with him, it becomes clear
to the reader what is going on (*CP&T* 244). Richard
Whittingham has been mistaken for Dick Whittington
(someone later asks him how his cat is getting on) and
has been admitted into a reunion of some of the
best-known characters from fairy-tales. Our literal-
minded narrator does not recognise this, and much of
the fun in the story comes from the reader's being able
to work out from the narrator's detailed, realistic but
uncomprehending descriptions who the various people
are. Cinderella, the Sleeping Beauty, Puss-in-Boots, Tom
Thumb, Beauty and the Beast, and many more, are
there. The hosts of the party are Bluebeard's surviving
wife and her second husband. The narrator's strange
experience ends with the appearance of a 'little old
lady, leaning on a thin wand'. All the characters greet
her in 'shrill, sweet voices', signalling that they belong
to the world of faery, and they call her 'Madame la
Féemarraine' (fairy godmother). Immediately afterwards the narrator finds himself lying in the wood
(*CP&T* 256–7). It is morning, and we can believe, if we
like, that he has been asleep and dreaming all night.

Richard Whittingham, pursuing his historical

research, can be seen as a representative of one part of Gaskell the writer – the careful, accurate social historian. He has known what Gaskell called the 'hidden world of art', but has grown out of it, as we see when he gets into a conversation about Jack the Giant-killer:

> Jack the Giant-killer had once, it is true, been rather an intimate friend of mine, as far as (printer's) ink and paper can keep up a friendship, but I had not heard his name mentioned for years; and for aught I knew he lay enchanted with King Arthur's knights, who lie entranced until the blast of the trumpets of four mighty kings shall call them to help at England's need. (253–4)

Like Gaskell, he has experienced the fascination of Arthur's hidden world, but he does not think of it as a realm he can re-enter. His relationship to and admiration for Calvin underlines his difference from the fairy-tale world. Significantly, he refers to Calvin as the 'Great Reformer'. Gaskell herself hoped in some way to be a reformer through her realistic writing, and in creating this narrator she is commenting on her own aspirations.

The story suggests two possible ways of responding to the characters Whittingham encounters in the château. In his account of them, the creatures of fairy-tale are comically diminished. They have apparently been stuck in the château since their creation by the French writers Charles Perrault, Madame de Beaumont and Madame d'Aulnoy in the seventeenth century. Their immortality does not include immunity to decay. Cinderella is 'a very sweet-looking lady, who must have been a great beauty in her youth', but she is now 'extremely fat' (245), and her feet, so swollen that she cannot walk, are taking revenge on her, she says, for forcing them into such tiny slippers in her youth. The romance belonging to the characters' original stories is fading faster than their looks, and the worldly-wise narrator describes them in a way that reduces them to mundane contemporaries. The Sleeping Beauty is introduced as a lady

> beautiful, splendid as the dawn, but – sound asleep on a magnificent settee. A gentleman who showed so much irritation at her ill-timed slumbers, that I think he must have been her husband, was trying to awaken her with actions not far removed from shakings. (249)

Other fairy-tale characters are shown similarly doomed to repeat gestures that have lost their original meaning. The story can be read as a witty, realistic glance at the fairy-tale world that finds it charming, but inadequate.

On the other hand, we might find the narrator's response itself inadequate. In a place where the reader of fairy-tales knows that magic and marvel exist, Whittingham can only find ordinary people. However, he is uneasily aware that he has no right to the welcome he is being given, suggesting that at some level he recognises that he has entered an enchanted world where he has no place. The appearance of Madame la Féemarraine at the end of the story hints at the limitations of the realistic picture the narrator has given us of the château's inhabitants. This is the climax of the short piece, revealing that it is fairy-land Whittingham has strayed into and simultaneously banishing him from it:

> And just as I spoke, the great folding-doors were thrown open wide, and every one started to their feet

to greet a little old lady, leaning on a thin, black wand – and –

'Madame la Féemarraine,' was announced by a chorus of sweet shrill voices.

And in a moment I was lying in the grass close by a hollow oak-tree . . . (256–7)

The fairy godmother, of course, is the benign if enigmatic ruling figure of one of the fairy-tales alluded to here, *Cinderella*. She rules the world of 'Curious, If True', commanding the allegiance of everyone in the château, and returning the narrator to the real world. She has sometimes been identified with Madame d'Aulnoy, writer of fairy-tales, but more helpful than a particular identification is the idea that Gaskell wants to give this enchanted world a female creator. Most of the tales to which she alludes in this story are versions written by a man, Charles Perrault, but they were popularly associated with female story-telling, having been published as *Tales of Mother Goose* with a frontispiece engraving of a woman telling stories to children.

The mother-figure who tells enchanting stories might be an appropriate image for Gaskell herself. Among her friends she was a famous story-teller from her girlhood. She particularly liked to tell tales of the supernatural, and 'no one ever came near her in the gift of telling a story', claimed Susanna Winkworth.[5] Later, Dickens associated her with a woman of legendary story-telling power when he called her 'my dear Scheherezade'.

In 'Curious, If True' the figure of the writer is split into the 'sensible and historical' but somewhat blinkered narrator Whittingham, and the old lady with a wand, who does not speak at all, but seems to be the source of the enchanted world that the narrator is trying to decipher. Here Gaskell is dramatising the

self-splitting that she had articulated ten years earlier
in her letter to Eliza Fox. The truth-seeking researcher,
whose pursuit of his connections with Calvin suggests
stern duty and self-denial, is imagined as male, just as
earlier, when writing *Mary Barton*, Gaskell had thought
of adopting a male pseudonym. Gaskell is here
imagining the artist split into masculine duty, feminine
pleasure; masculine reality, feminine fantasy.

However, the split between Richard Whittingham
and the fairy-tale world that he visits is far from total.
When he wakes up back in reality, it feels like anything
but a banishment:

> I was lying in the grass close by a hollow oak-tree,
> with the slanting glory of the dawning day shining
> full in my face, and thousands of little birds and
> delicate insects piping and warbling out their
> welcome to the ruddy splendour. (257)

Reality itself has become enchanting through the
experience of the fantasy world. The misanthropic
Whittingham, who only explored the countryside
because he wanted to avoid his unprepossessing fellow
guests (241), has been altered by his experience in the
château. He has refused to adopt the cynical approach
to its inhabitants displayed by one of the fairy-tale
characters himself, M. Poucet (hero of the tale of the
seven-league boots), and he has been given a vision.
During his time in the château, he looks out of the
window, back into the wood where he lost his way, and
sees the ghost of a little peasant girl who is said to have
been eaten by a wolf. This, of course, is Red Riding
Hood, who in Perrault's version of her story is not
rescued by the woodcutter. In death she is reconciled
with her killer, for she appears with the wolf, which
seems to be 'licking her hand, as if in penitent love'

(254). Red Riding Hood then has a peculiar status: having died in a fairy-tale, she is a ghost to a world that is itself a fantasy. She seems doubly removed from reality, yet she is also used as an image of ordinary country life, 'a little girl, with the "capuchon" on, that takes the place of a peasant girl's bonnet in France' (254). The narrator's companion at the window (Beauty from *Beauty and the Beast*) exclaims:

> There, we have seen her! . . . Though so long dead, her simple story of household goodness and trustful simplicity still lingers in the hearts of all who have ever heard of her; and the country-people about here say that seeing that phantom-child on this anniversary brings good luck for the year. Let us hope that we shall share in the traditionary good fortune.
>
> (254-5)

This phantom-child recalls not only Red Riding Hood but Wordsworth's Lucy Grey, the lost child who can still be seen tripping along in the lonesome wild. The good fortune that the sight of her brings is a very Wordsworthian blessing; Whittingham's return to the real world with 'the slanting glory of the dawning day shining full in [his] face' (257) is like a restoration of the 'visionary gleam' whose loss is lamented in the Immortality Ode.

The narrator's experience of the fantastic, then, has sent him back to the real world with a renewed sense of wonder in everyday reality. Here is an imaginative resolution to Gaskell's sense of artistic split. The real, but enchanting world Whittingham returns to can be compared with the world Gaskell creates in late works such as 'Cousin Phillis' and *Wives and Daughters*, works that present as their reality the natural beauty of the countryside and the 'household goodness and trustful simplicity' of young women like Phillis Holman and Molly Gibson, and invest that reality with a sense of wonder that is Gaskell's legacy from a lifetime of excursions into her 'hidden world of art'.

Wordswortḥ s 'Lucy' poems, with their idea of the young woman as 'child of nature', are often brought to mind in Gaskell's later work. Lucy is alluded to in connection with both Phillis Holman and Molly Gibson: the narrator of 'Cousin Phillis' quotes two lines from 'She dwelt among th'untrodden ways' in evocation of the heroine, while in *Wives and Daughters* the heroine herself feels, at one point, that she is being 'rolled round in earth's diurnal course,/with rocks, and stones, and trees' like Lucy in 'A Slumber did My Spirit Seal'. It is worth considering Gaskell's use of Lucy figures in the light of recent feminist criticism of the Lucy poems. Lucy is sometimes a child (as in 'Lucy Grey') and sometimes the poet's lover (as in 'Strange Fits of Passion I have known'), and sometimes she is unnamed (as in 'A Slumber did My Spirit Seal'), but she is always associated with loss. Either she is dead or (as in 'Strange Fits of Passion') the threat of her death hangs over the poet. As Meena Alexander explains, 'Whether adult or child, named or nameless, she is bound to the natural landscape. She crystallises loss, intense longing. She is the impossible object of the poet's desire, an iconic representation of the Romantic feminine.'[6] In losing Lucy, and thus his own connection with the feminine nature he so desires, the poet gains a major theme for his Romantic writing, and a place in masculine culture. He writes about her loss. Mary Jacobus, pointing out that in 'Three years she grew' Lucy becomes a part of the landscape, adds that her death and assimilation into nature enable the poet to assume his identity:

Lucy here is not just a memory; she becomes the ground or background for Wordsworthian figuration. He writes on her. However loving, all acts of naming or poetic naming such as those lavished on Lucy might be said to involve the constitution of the speaking or writing subject at the expense of the silenced object.[7]

The male narrator's experience in 'Curious, If True' is comparable to that of the Romantic poet as described by Alexander and Jacobus. His vision of the lost Lucy figure frees his creative imagination, allowing him to become more than merely 'sensible and historical' (249), and able to write of enchantment.

If Whittingham, like the Romantic poet, depends on the icon of the innocent, dead young female for the grounding of his creativity, where does that leave Gaskell, who is, I have suggested, using his story as a way of dramatising her concerns about her own creative role? She, too, might be said to be gaining her creative identity through the objectification and silencing of the Lucy figure. There is, however, a difference. Gaskell is not to be identified with Whittingham; rather the story contains projections of two aspects of her creative personality. She is equally to be found in Madame la Féemarraine. The parable is not about the birth of a Romantic poet but about the renewal of a realistic prose writer; and the emphasis is not on the loss of the Lucy figure but on her re-discovery. Only by being reminded of the everyday enchantment of her household goodness can the sensible writer gain a poetic sense of the real world where he belongs.

'Curious, If True' is thus a transposition of the story of the Romantic poet's development onto the concerns of the Victorian novelist. In so far as Gaskell uses the story as a way of resolving her own artistic conflicts by constructing an aesthetic in which Wordsworthian nature, fairy-tale enchantment and realistic narrative can harmoniously combine, she, like the male poet, depends on the icon of the lost female. Yet in the mature work that follows this story, Gaskell uses her new aesthetic confidence to rescue the Lucy figure from silence and death. 'Cousin Phillis' and *Wives and Daughters* both return to the figure of the innocent young female, but in these narratives she is not lost or silenced. Unlike the male Romantic poet, the female Victorian novelist is interested in 'Lucy's' subjectivity and survival. These late works resist the sacrifice of the young woman. Gaskell's last heroines are like Lucy, but a Lucy with a difference.

Paul, the narrator of 'Cousin Phillis', compares Phillis – without realising it – to Wordsworth's Lucy.

My cousin Phillis was like a rose that had come to full bloom on the sunny side of a lonely house, sheltered from storms. I have read in some book of poetry –

A maid whom there were none to praise,
    And very few to love.

And somehow those lines always reminded me of Phillis; yet they were not true of her either. I never heard her praised; and out of her own household there were very few to love her; but though no one spoke out their approbation, she always did right in her parents' eyes, out of her natural simple goodness and wisdom. (*CCP* 289–90)

Phillis, like Lucy, is compared to a sheltered flower; but she is not completely the secluded child of nature. Her world, however small, is a social world of parents and household, and her relationship is to the social world, whereas Lucy exists only in nature and for the poet who writes of her. Paul's relationship to Phillis is like and unlike Wordsworth's to Lucy. Like, because he creates her story in his words, and because she represents for him a lost world of harmony with the natural. His first sight of her is so vivid in his memory that it remains a living vision: 'I see her now – cousin Phillis' (226). As the Wordsworth of the Lucy poems may be said to be creating himself as poetic subject in writing on Lucy, so Paul is writing of his own coming into manhood as he narrates his cousin's story. The first two pages of the story are devoted to recollections of Paul's first job, first lodgings away from home and his relationship with his father. After mentioning a family dispute of later years, when Paul 'really offended against [his] father's sense of right' (221), an incident never further explained, the narrator suddenly re-collects that he is supposed to be writing about cousin Phillis, not himself. It still takes a few more pages before he gets to her. Even then Phillis's story is occasionally interrupted by references to Paul's, and we learn, in passing, about his meeting with his own future wife.

Yet Paul's relationship to Phillis is unlike Words-worth's to Lucy because it is not exclusive. Instead of being the only one to appreciate her, he is an onlooker on the intense drama of her relationships with her father, Minister Holman, and Edward Holdsworth. Holdsworth, the managing engineer for the new railway line between Eltham and Hornby, disrupts the Holmans' quiet, pastoral existence with his talk of modern technology and foreign countries. He loves Phillis but leaves her for a chance to further his career in Canada. The pathos and necessity of cultural change is a familiar Gaskellian theme, and the railway a common Victorian figure for all that is modern. In 'Cousin Phillis', though, social transformation is mainly there as a metaphor for personal changes. The railway is not in itself a threat. Holman has built a life combining Christianity, strong family ties, classical learning and consciously Virgilian agricultural labour. He is quite capable of absorbing technological advances into his rounded existence, as his enthusiasm for Paul's father's invention shows; but his daughter's growth to maturity is another matter. Holman's idyll depends on the presence of a daughter to share the intellectual pleasures that his wife cannot understand. Phillis is infantilised, wearing childish pinafores at an age when other girls have given them up; her Lucy-like seclusion is unnaturally induced. When she falls in love with Holdsworth her father's dreams are shattered.

Phillis's lover and father both think of her as an unconscious innocent. Holdsworth, leaving for Canada, compares her to Sleeping Beauty and imagines that he will return in a couple of years to wake her to love. Because he has not told her of his love he does not feel any guilt when he marries another woman instead – another Lucy figure, 'Lucille, the second daughter . . . curiously like Phillis Holman' as he tells Paul in his letter (291). Lucille is clearly a substitute not just for Phillis herself but, through her friendly, rural yet cultured family, for the ideal pastoral existence represented for Holdsworth by the Holmans. When Phillis's father finds out about her heartbreak he blames Paul for telling Phillis about Holdsworth's love. To him his daughter is 'So young, so pure from the world! how could you go and talk to such a child, raising hopes, exciting feelings' (307). Her declaration that he is wrong, that she loved Holdsworth before Paul spoke, is the crisis point for both of them. The stress of revealing her sexual feelings to a father who feels betrayed by their existence brings on a collapse and a long illness.

Phillis's sexuality is pinpointed as the element neither father nor lover can incorporate into their idealised visions of her. The Lucy figure is revealed as a masculine fantasy based on seclusion of and total possession of the desired object. The logic of the narrative would seem to support Brother Robinson's stern admonition as he tells the anxious father to examine 'whether you have not made an idol of your daughter?'; but the brethren's punitive theology is rejected. Gaskell holds with Holman, who 'hold[s] with Christ that afflictions are not sent by God in wrath as penalties for sin' (313); and Phillis recovers. Unlike Lucy, she is not dead or lost. For all the intense nostalgia of the narrative tone when first introducing Phillis, Phillis at the end of Paul's narrative is still a presence in his life. The words that describe her as changed also indicate her survival into the narrative's present: 'I sometimes grew desponding, and feared that she would never be what she had been before; no more she has, in some ways' (316).

The ending of the story achieves a fine balance between the pathos of Phillis's illusory hope that she can 'go back to the peace of the old days' (317), and the reader's understanding that her efforts to take the servant Betty's good advice, and do something for herself, may enable her to go forward into a changing world. At one point Gaskell thought of spelling out more of Phillis's future, having her carry out drainage work in the village.[8] Thus she would have become a moderniser like Holdsworth, but with more care for the people's existing way of life. This union of social and personal development, and representation of a woman grown up into public action, was probably rejected as too schematic: the later ending is effective in its open-endedness. There is just the hint of a wider life for Phillis, a 'change of thought and scene' (317).

The father–daughter relationship that is prominent in 'Cousin Phillis' is more extensively treated in *Wives and Daughters*. Gaskell's last novel depicts country-town life in the 1820s, and shows her usual interest in the assimilation of social and cultural change into traditional rural life. The changing position of the aristocratic Cumnor family and the rising importance of professional men like Mr Gibson and the scientific explorer Roger Hamley are chronicled. Although there is much affection for past ways in the chapters on Molly's childhood, and there is an idyllic quality about her first visit to Hamley Hall, the work is not nostalgic about old England. The Miss Brownings, old-fashioned spinsters a little reminiscent of the *Cranford* ladies, do not have the charm or the moral strength of those earlier characters. If there is a wistful looking-back, it is not so much to the old way of life before the Reform Bill and the railways, as it is to an imagined moment of hope and promise, when old ways are about to change. Roger, for all his background in the squirearchy and his father's pride in the ancient Hamley name, is a man of the future, and Mr Gibson wishes he belonged to the younger generation so that he could witness more of the scientific progress that is beginning to gather momentum. *Wives and Daughters* takes its rural society to the threshold of the Victorian age, and its view of the changing world is often optimistic: greater knowledge and a degree of democracy seem to be waiting gently round the corner. The main focus, though, is on woman's place in the new world: specifically, on how Molly Gibson can find a place to grow up into.

It is a moot point whether Molly will be allowed to grow up: her father, like Phillis's, wants to keep his daughter a child. Molly's mother died when the child was three, and Mr Gibson has brought her up with the help of a maid and a governess. For all the bracing banter of his conversations with his daughter, he would clearly like to protect her from life and experience. Only half-joking, he tells the puzzled governess:

> Don't teach Molly too much: she must sew, and read, and write, and do her sums; but I want to keep her a child, and if I find more learning desirable for her, I'll see about giving it to her myself. After all, I am not sure that reading or writing is necessary. . . . however we must yield to the prejudices of society, Miss Eyre, and so you may teach the child to read.
>
> (WD 32)

When Molly reaches puberty his anxieties intensify. Panic-stricken when one of his medical pupils tries to send her a love-letter, Mr Gibson sends her on a visit to Mrs Hamley, and starts looking for a suitable chaperon for her – actions that bring about a chain of ironic consequences. At Hamley Hall Molly meets Roger, the man she is to love, and Osborne, in whose secret marriage she becomes involved as confidante; while Mr Gibson's second marriage, undertaken mainly for Molly's sake, nearly estranges him from his jealous daughter, and provides as her female guide and protector a scheming matchmaker, compounded of all the feminine wiles Mr Gibson detests, and from which Molly herself is singularly free.

The contrast between Molly and Cynthia Kirkpatrick, her stepsister, defines the heroine's peculiar goodness. Cynthia, flirtatious and fascinating, is very sympathetically created: her charm is believable, her affection for Molly is real, and her shortcomings are traced to a childhood starved of love. Nevertheless, she functions to highlight by contrast Molly's integrity and deeper response to life. Molly is household goodness and trustful simplicity personified, and she is the ideal daughter not only for Mr Gibson but for Squire and Mrs Hamley, who almost adopt her when she goes to stay with them. A daughter's life seems, at first, a very peaceful one:

> Her days at Hamley were well filled up with the small duties that would have belonged to a daughter of the house had there been one. She made breakfast for the lonely squire, and would willingly have carried up madam's, but that daily piece of work belonged to the squire, and was jealously guarded by him. She read the smaller print of the newspapers aloud to him, city articles, money and corn-markets included. She strolled about the gardens with him, gathering fresh flowers, meanwhile, to deck the drawing-room against Mrs Hamley should come down. She was her companion when she took her drives in the close carriage; they read poetry and mild literature together in Mrs Hamley's sitting-room upstairs. She was quite clever at cribbage now, and could beat the squire if she took pains. (WD 82)

The affectionate glow surrounding Molly's Hamley life does not quite blot out its monotony; and soon there is evidence that the duties of a daughter can stifle her completely. When Roger Hamley advises Molly to think of her father rather than herself, and accept his new marriage, she rebels in word if not in deed:

> It will be very dull when I shall have killed myself, as it were, and live only in trying to do, and to be, as

other people like. I don't see any end to it. I might as well never have lived. (139)

Much of the narrative is concerned with Molly's struggle to put this programme into operation. Dutifully suppressing her own feelings, she welcomes her stepmother and even gives her the name once reserved for 'mamma'. She submits to the new Mrs Gibson's comic endeavours to prove herself a good stepmother by generously refurnishing Molly's room, and in the process threatening precious childhood memories. She spends much of her energy keeping other people's sexual secrets – Cynthia's entanglement with Mr Preston and Osborne's marriage to Aimée – while her own erotic life remains a secret to her own consciousness. Evidently loving Roger but having no idea of it herself, Molly may seem to be an example of Gaskell taking the Victorian heroine's innocence a little too far; but her underlying theme is the danger to Molly of such innocence. Admiring selflessness, Gaskell nevertheless presents Molly's self-suppression as potentially fatal to her.

While the social comedy of Hollingford life trots on undisturbed, Molly, unnoticed, goes through a series of crises and gives up practically everything she loves. She relinquishes her father to his new wife, and Roger to Cynthia. When Mrs Hamley, more of a second mother to her than Mrs Gibson, is dying, she no longer asks for Molly, and Molly quietly withdraws from the family when she can no longer be useful. Eventually, after Osborne's death, Molly helps establish his wife and son at Hamley Hall, replacing herself, the squire's substitute daughter, with the true daughter-in-law he must learn to recognise. After this final act of self-effacement Molly falls ill: the physical cause is given as

her exhaustion after nursing Mrs Osborne Hamley, but
she has been slowly killing herself all along.

It is when Roger and Cynthia get engaged that
Molly's self-abnegation is imaged in a way that associates her with Wordsworth's Lucy.

> She felt as if she could not understand it all; but as
> for that matter, what could she understand? Nothing.
> For a few minutes her brain seemed in too great a
> whirl to comprehend anything but that she was
> being carried on in earth's diurnal course, with rocks,
> and stones, and trees, with as little volition on her
> part as if she were dead. (391)

Like Lucy she is reduced to being a part of the earth,
but there is a difference: while the poem imagines the
lost Lucy, Gaskell's narrative is about what it feels like
to be Lucy. Restoring 'Lucy' to subjectivity, Gaskell
undoes her death. Molly's loss of self is only
temporary. The passage continues:

> Then the room grew stifling, and instinctively she
> went to the open casement window, and leant out,
> gasping for breath. Gradually the consciousness of
> the soft peaceful landscape stole into her mind, and
> stilled the buzzing confusion. There, bathed in the
> almost level rays of the autumn sunlight, lay the
> landscape she had known and loved from childhood;
> as quiet, as full of low humming life as it had been at
> this hour for many generations. (391)

Molly recovers herself as a human subject looking on
nature. She is not an inanimate part of the landscape
but someone who can read the landscape, which
connects her to her individual past and the past life of
her society. This is one indication that Molly will not

take self-abnegation too far: she will refuse Lucy's position, and survive.

The story of Molly's developing selflessness is counterpointed by instances where she asserts her own right to judge and act. Ironically, it is in her selfless service to Cynthia, her unacknowledged rival, that Molly is most able to assert herself. Protecting her stepsister against her father, she briefly becomes a rebellious (but guiltless) daughter herself. When she meets Preston to return Cynthia's letters, her father is horrified. It seems to him that Molly has entered a clandestine relationship like the one he prevented Mr Coxe from initiating. This time, though, Molly turns the tables on her father, demanding from him the same kind of unquestioning trust she had given him when he refused to explain why he was sending her to Hamley. She agrees that she has met Preston, refuses to say why and will not let him talk to Preston to find out the truth. The moment when her father agrees to trust her and to do as she suggests marks the point of Molly's growing up.

Gaskell is a little over-insistent on Molly's heroism in the Preston affair. In the confrontation with her father her face is 'white, but it [bears] the impress of the final sincerity of death, when the true expression prevails without the poor disguises of time' (544). Preston himself seems to be defeated simply by her purity: he realises he must stop persecuting Cynthia immediately after noticing 'that Molly was as unconscious that he was a young man, and she a young woman, as if she had been a pure angel of heaven' (507). In passages like this Molly almost becomes that cliché of Victorian fiction, the sexless young woman-angel. Gaskell is searching here for a rhetoric to transform the conventional innocent heroine from a figure of pathos to one of power: a representative of truth. Molly's father once compares her to Spenser's Una (54), while Roger describes Cynthia as 'the false Duessa' (677). Molly is seen as the bearer of an ideal steadfastness and truth into the ordinary social world of nineteenth-century England. In creating her Gaskell is attempting to restore an older signification of the figure of the virgin as a bearer of power: she wants to change Lucy back into Una. This is in line with Victorian interest in Una, who often figures in nineteenth-century illustrations of *The Faerie Queene*. However, Gaskell does not use the figure of Una, any more than that of Lucy, without revising its significance. Spenser's Una is defined in opposition to Duessa, whose foulness and falseness she exposes. The figure corresponding to Duessa in *Wives and Daughters* is changeable Cynthia; but Molly acts to help Cynthia to conceal evidence of her fickle nature from judgemental men. Her involvement in the Preston affair is motivated by a desire to shield Cynthia from exposure. This sisterly solidarity does not sully Molly's Una-like truth, for Cynthia is not really a Duessa: she only appears so to disappointed men. Roger himself realises this when he withdraws his application of the name to her: 'If I called her the false Duessa it was because I wanted to express my sense of the difference between her and Molly as strongly as I could' (677). The absolute division of women into pure and impure, true and false, is seen in this novel to be the work of biased men. Molly is better than Cynthia but not her opposite: the Una/Duessa contrast is replaced by loving sisterhood.

Once Molly's father's trust in her is established, the other consequences of her meetings with Preston soon fade into insignificance. Molly suffers for a while from Hollingford gossip, but her reputation is easily and comically retrieved by Lady Harriet, who makes sure she is seen in Hollingford with Molly, knowing that this aristocratic patronage is enough to prove Molly's virtue to the local ladies. Here, as elsewhere in the novel, the aristocrats act as guardians to the middle-class protagonists. The older generation of Cumnors rule, or think they rule, the lives of their inferiors: Lady Cumnor, for example, calmly deciding that her former governess should marry the local doctor. The younger generation, represented by Lord Hollingford and Lady Harriet, are beginning to work out a new relation to the middle classes. Hollingford is a patron to scientists without considering himself superior to them. Lady Harriet, somewhat wryly, acknowledges Molly's moral (if not social) equality with her, and Molly's ability to tell Lady Harriet unpleasant truths wins her respect. Lady Harriet is, indeed, well aware of the aristocracy's changing position, and realises that the Cumnors have become 'a show and a spectacle': they must now earn their tenants' votes by putting on a performance of aristocratic splendour at local functions (309). She and Lord Hollingford retain some power, but it is a diminishing, and to some extent a fanciful one, as we see in the episode where the aristocratic brother and sister speculate on a possible marriage between Molly and Roger. Lady Harriet comments, 'we are like the genie and the fairy in the *Arabian Nights' Entertainment*, who each cried up the merits of the Prince Caramal-zaman and the Princess Badoura' (654). It is a fitting image of the aristocracy's new function in this novel: still having, or imagining themselves to have, authorial control over other people's stories, but no longer protagonists of a story of their own. Molly and Roger's relationship (clearly intended to end in marriage) may be helped along by these benign aristocrats but it is essentially independent of them.

Wives and Daughters, then, subscribes to a myth of harmonious social change, in which the aristocracy gradually and gracefully resigns its hegemony to the professional middle classes. Gentle improvement is also expected in Molly's life. In the new world of meritocracy and scientific progress looked forward to in this novel, Gaskell optimistically sees the household goodness of her heroine surviving. Molly is not sacrificed. Her goodness and simplicity are combined with independent judgement, and, increasingly, a recognised role in Hollingford society. The later episodes bring her rewards: her father's recognition of her right to judge and act for herself; evidence of Cynthia's real affection for her; a certain amount of admiration from the Cumnors and their friends; and, eventually, Roger Hamley's love. The whole of the final movement of the novel could be summed up in the title of chapter 54: 'Molly Gibson's Worth is Discovered'. Unlike Phillis, Molly never reaches any sexual aware-ness: in the novel as we have it she remains comically unaware that her feelings for Roger encompass any-thing but friendship. Clearly, though, they were meant to marry eventually, and the path is smoothed for their union. Mr Gibson, with more insight into his own feelings than Minister Holman, has already mentally resigned her to Roger: '"Lover *versus* father!" thought he, half sadly. "Lover wins"' (679).

Roger Hamley is the new, scientific man, and Molly the new woman who, only half-educated herself, is intelligent and, as Lady Harriet insists, 'is capable of appreciating him' (654). It is a disappointing goal for a young woman whose growth to maturity and moral responsibility has been so compellingly traced. In *Wives and Daughters*, a daughter's only fulfilment seems to be in becoming a wife. Gaskell here shows little interest in women's movement into the public sphere, though this issue entered some of her earlier novels, and certainly concerned her on a personal level as her own daughters grew up (Meta at one point decided to train as a nurse, and had her parents' support). It would be a mistake, though, to judge Gaskell's last novel on these grounds. She has deliberately confined herself to an examination of women's role as 'relative creatures', asking whether a woman can live the traditional feminine life without being either an untrustworthy exploiter of feminine charm (as Mrs Gibson and Cynthia, in their different ways, both are) or a victim, overcome by being devoted entirely to others. She answers in the affirmative, but only just. Mrs Hamley is such a victim, and Molly only narrowly escapes becoming one.[9] Gaskell's optimistic conclusion about Molly is perhaps a tender fantasy about a daughter-heroine. The violet half-hidden in the shade is brought out to be admired, and the maid whom there were very few to love is given the affections of the whole cast of the novel's characters – and of the novel's readers.

Gaskell's work does to some extent contribute to the comforting Victorian myth that society will gradually and harmoniously improve. It is this optimism, perhaps, that has made critics, even when they admire her, persist in denying her entrance to the select society of Victorian 'great writers'. The criticism is sometimes put in terms of her inability to confront and convey evil: a 'dynamic drive' is lacking because she 'finds it difficult to think of anyone as actively bad', and cannot present 'the full creation of unpleasant characters or the free play of evil'.[10] Gaskell, it would seem, is just too nice. She is, however, a more challenging writer than this suggests. The position that allows her to write optimistically about her society also allows her to make subtle revisions to its codes.

The divided and hesitant writer of Gaskell's early career, conscious of a split between a woman's duties and an artist's, a moralist's and an enchanter's, evolved into the assured creator of the late stories and *Wives and Daughters*. The new confidence depended on an imaginative act of reconciliation between the warring members of the self. Perhaps such a reconciliation can only be incomplete and precarious, and it may have to be bought at the cost of smoothing over real and significant anxieties. It would be possible to prefer the early Gaskell, painfully conscious of social injustice, who doubted her right to have a big house in Manchester and live as an artist, to the later writer who found a way to live that life. Yet what she achieved as an artist remains important. She subtly alters myths, stock figures and poetic types to accommodate a woman-centred viewpoint. The polar opposition of Una and Duessa is broken down when Gaskell writes from Una's viewpoint. Lucy is restored to subjectivity. Making use of a Wordsworthian view of the healing powers of nature for the artist, but in the process offering a critique of it; making a broadly optimistic analysis of social development but still asking difficult questions about women's agency within her society – Gaskell becomes an unemphatic but significant practitioner of what Adrienne Rich calls 'writing as re-vision'.[11]

Notes

Notes to Chapter 1

1. Lord David Cecil's discussion of Gaskell in *Early Victorian Novelists* (London: Constable, 1934) is a notorious example of devaluing a writer by reference to her femininity: 'she was all a woman was expected to be; gentle, domestic, tactful, unintellectual, prone to tears, easily shocked. So far from chafing at the limits imposed on her activities, she accepted them with serene satisfaction' (p. 198). The first writer to give extended treatment to Gaskell's involvement in feminism is Aina Rubenius in *The Woman Question in Mrs Gaskell's Life and Work* (Uppsala: Lundequistka Bokhandeln, 1950).

2. Raymond Williams finds that despite her 'deep imaginative sympathy' for the workers, Gaskell in *Mary Barton* shares and expresses middle-class fears about working-class action. *Culture and Society* (London: Chatto, 1958) p. 90. John Lucas writes that the reconciliation between classes in *North and South* comes down to teaching the lower orders to know their place. 'Mrs Gaskell and Brotherhood', in *Tradition and Tolerance in Nineteenth-century Fiction*, ed. David Howard *et al.* (London: Routledge and Kegan Paul, 1966) p. 205.

3. See especially Patsy Stoneman, *Elizabeth Gaskell* (Brighton: Harvester, 1987), and Margaret Homans, *Bearing the Word: Language and Female Experience in Nineteenth-century Women's Writing* (Chicago: University of Chicago Press, 1986).

4. Winifred Gérin, *Elizabeth Gaskell: A Biography* (Oxford: Oxford University Press, 1976) p. 17.

5. Annette B. Hopkins, *Elizabeth Gaskell: Her Life and Work* (London: John Lehmann, 1932) p. 34.

6. See Sally Stonehouse, 'A Letter from Mrs Gaskell', *Brontë Society Transactions*, vol. 20 (1991) pp. 217–22; and J. A. V. Chapple, 'Two Unpublished Gaskell Letters from Burrow Hall, Lancashire', *The Gaskell Society Journal*, vol. 6 (1992) pp. 67–72.

7. W. R. Greg, *Edinburgh Review* (April 1849) pp. 402–35.

8. Elizabeth Gaskell, *My Lady Ludlow and Other Stories* (Oxford: World's Classics, 1989) p. 131.

9. John Ruskin, 'Of Queens' Gardens', in *Sesame and Lilies* (1865; rpt. London: George Allen, 1901) p. 108.

10. Ibid., p. 186.

11. Françoise Basch, *Relative Creatures: Victorian Women in Society and the Novel* (London, 1974) pp. 7, 269.

12. Nancy Armstrong, *Desire and Domestic Fiction: A Political History of the Novel* (Oxford: Oxford University Press, 1987) pp. 28-58.

13. [J. Ludlow], *North British Review*, vol. 19 (May 1853) pp. 167-9.

14. Ibid., p. 169.

15. Ibid., p. 155.

16. Ibid., pp. 162, 163.

17. Homans, *Bearing the Word*, p. 11.

18. Ibid., p. 13.

19. Ibid., p. 38.

20. Armstrong, *Desire and Domestic Fiction*, p. 26.

21. Ibid., p. 163.

22. Homans, *Bearing the Word*, p. 226.

23. Woolf writes: 'if one is a woman one is often surprised by a sudden splitting off of consciousness, say in walking down Whitehall, when from being the natural inheritor of that civilization, she becomes, on the contrary, outside of it, alien and critical' – *A Room of One's Own* (St Albans: Panther, 1977) p. 93.

Notes to Chapter 2

1. For example, Manchester's Unitarian MPs and manufacturers opposed factory legislation intended to limit employers' powers. See Valentine Cunningham, *Everywhere Spoken Against: Dissent in the Victorian Novel* (Oxford: Clarendon Press, 1975) pp. 132-3.

2. See Monica Fryckstedt, *Elizabeth Gaskell's* Mary Barton *and* Ruth: *A Challenge to Christian England* (Uppsala: Almquist and Wiksell, 1982) pp. 88-94.

3. W. Greg, *Edinburgh Review*, vol. 89 (1849) pp. 402-35. This review is discussed in Cunningham, *Everywhere Spoken Against*, pp. 133-5.

4. M. Hompes, 'Mrs E. C. Gaskell', *Gentleman's Magazine*, vol. 55 (1895) p. 124.

5. See *Westminster and Foreign Quarterly Review*, vol. 51 (1849) pp. 48-63, and *British Quarterly Review*, vol. 9 (1849) pp. 117-36.

6. Carlyle, 'Chartism', in *Critical and Miscellaneous Essays* (London: Chapman and Hall, 1899) vol. IV, p. 169.

7. See John Lucas, 'Mrs Gaskell and Brotherhood', in *Tradition and Tolerance in Nineteenth-century Fiction*, ed. David Howard *et al.* (London: Routledge and Kegan Paul) p. 167.

8. Carlyle, 'Corn-Law Rhymes' (1839); in *Critical and Miscellaneous Essays*, vol. III, p. 138.

9. Ibid., 148.

10. The theme of women's public speaking is treated by Rosemarie Bodenheimer in 'Private Grief and Public Acts in *Mary Barton*', *Dickens Studies Annual*, vol. 9 (1981) 195–216.

11. Elizabeth Haldane, *Mrs Gaskell and Her Friends* (London: Hodder and Stoughton, 1931) pp. 47–8.

12. John Rylands Library, English Mss 730, 14.

13. Craig Owens, 'The Discourse of Others: Feminists and Postmodernism', in *Postmodern Culture*, ed. Hal Foster (London and Sydney: Pluto Press, 1985) pp. 68–9.

14. This point is made by W. A. Craik, who argues that in *Mary Barton* Gaskell needs 'the social aim' less for its own sake than in order 'to justify writing at all'. See *Elizabeth Gaskell and the English Provincial Novel* (London: Methuen, 1975) p. 4.

Notes to Chapter 3

1. *Sharpe's London Magazine*, vol. 2 (1853) p. 126.

2. See *Spectator*, Saturday, 15 January 1853, pp. 61–2.

3. *Sharpe's London Magazine*, vol. 2 (1853) p. 126.

4. Letter to Gaskell, 26 April 1852. *The Brontës, Their Lives, Friendships and Correspondence*, ed. T. J. Wise and J. A. Symington (Oxford: Blackwell, 1933) vol. III, p. 332.

5. Letter to Blanche Smith, 19 April 1853, in *The Correspondence of Arthur Hugh Clough*, ed. Frederick Mulhauser (Oxford: Clarendon Press, 1957) vol. II, p. 418.

6. Brian Crick, 'Mrs Gaskell's *Ruth*: A Reconsideration', *Mosaic*, vol. 9 (1977) no. 2, pp. 85–104.

7. Alan Shelston, '*Ruth*: Mrs Gaskell's Neglected Novel', *Bulletin of the John Rylands Library*, vol. 58 (1975–6) pp. 182.

8. See Patsy Stoneman, *Elizabeth Gaskell* (Brighton: Harvester, 1987) p. 106.

9. Letter to Gaskell, 12 January 1853. In *The Brontës*, vol. IV, p. 34.

10. [J. M. Ludlow] *North British Review*, vol. 19 (1853) p. 169.

11. Elizabeth Rigby, '*Vanity Fair* and *Jane Eyre*', *Quarterly Review*, vol. 84 (1848) p. 174; Matthew Arnold, letter to Mrs Forster, 14 April 1853, in *Letters of Matthew Arnold 1848–1888*, ed. George W. E. Russell (London: Macmillan, 1895) vol. I, p. 29.

12. *The Brontës*, vol. IV, pp. 14 and 34–6.

13. Martineau's review of *Villette* for *Daily News*, quoted in *LCB*, p. 619.

14. *The Brontës*, vol. IV, pp. 76–7.

15. Ibid. vol. IV, p. 34.

16. Miriam J. Benn, 'Some Unpublished Gaskell Letters', *Notes and Queries*, vol. 225 (1980) p. 508.

17. Alan Shelston, notes to *LCB*, p. 592.

18. Winifred Gérin, *Charlotte Brontë: The Evolution of Genius* (Oxford: Clarendon, 1967) p. 573.

Notes to Chapter 4

1. Patsy Stoneman, *Elizabeth Gaskell* (Brighton: Harvester, 1987) p. 93.

2. See Nina Auerbach, *Communities of Women: An Idea in Fiction* (Cambridge, Mass.: Harvard University Press, 1978).

3. Martin Dodsworth, 'Women Without Men at Cranford', *Essays in Criticism*, vol. 13 (1963) pp. 132–45.

4. For a discussion of *North and South* as a novel challenging the paternalism initially embodied by the Hale family, see Rosemarie Bodenheimer, *The Politics of Story in Victorian Fiction* (Ithaca: Cornell University Press, 1988) pp. 53–67. Bodenheimer sees Gaskell's novel as in part an answer to Charlotte Brontë's *Shirley* (1849), arguing that 'If Brontë rests, finally, in the model of paternalism, Gaskell takes the parental metaphor apart to observe its absurdities and insists on the health of ideological change' (54).

5. This is argued in Deidre David, *Fictions of Resolution in Three Victorian Novels* (New York: Columbia University Press, 1981) pp. 43–4.

6. P. N. Furbank, 'Mendacity in Mrs Gaskell', *Encounter*, vol. 40 (1973) p. 51.

7. See Nancy Armstrong, *Desire and Domestic Fiction: A Political History of the Novel* (Oxford: Oxford University Press, 1987) pp. 42–8.

Notes to Chapter 5

1. Gaskell used Admiralty records of these incidents. For a discussion of her sources see A. W. Ward (ed.), *The Works of Mrs Gaskell*, vol. 6: *Sylvia's Lovers* (London: John Murray, 1920) pp. xxii–xxvi.

2. John McVeagh, *Elizabeth Gaskell* (London: Routledge and Kegan Paul, 1970) p. 45.

3. The letter is addressed to Marianne Gaskell, asking her to copy and send the critique to the novelist. Margaret Homans suggests that Marianne herself was the author of *The Three Paths*, but does not offer evidence for this view; see *Bearing the Word: Language and Female Experience in Nineteenth-century Women's Writing* (Chicago: University of Chicago Press, 1986) p. 171.

4. Thomas Macaulay, quoted in Rosemary Jann, *The Art and Science of Victorian History* (Columbus: Ohio State University Press, 1985) p. 71.

5. See Patsy Stoneman, *Elizabeth Gaskell* (Brighton: Harvester, 1987) p. 154.

6. J. Rignall, 'The Historical Double: *Waverley, Sylvia's Lovers, The Trumpet-Major*', *Essays in Criticism*, vol. 34 (1984) p. 23.

7. Ibid., p. 24.

8. The epigraph to *Sylvia's Lovers* is taken from *In Memoriam*, section LVI. Lines 25–8 of this section are:

> 'O life as futile, then, as frail!
>   O for thy voice to soothe and bless!
>   What hope of answer, or redress?
> Behind the veil, behind the veil.

Gaskell's epigraph comprises the last three lines of this quatrain, omitting mention of the troubling idea of life's futility.

Notes to Chapter 6

1. Edgar Wright, *Mrs Gaskell: The Basis for Reassessment* (London: Oxford University Press, 1965) p. 246.

2. Ibid., pp. 47, 196.

3. Patsy Stoneman, *Elizabeth Gaskell* (Brighton: Harvester, 1987) p. 201.

4. Angus Easson, *Elizabeth Gaskell* (London, Boston and Henley: Routledge and Kegan Paul, 1979) p. 220.

5. Quoted in A. B. Hopkins, *Elizabeth Gaskell: Her Life and Work* (London: John Lehmann, 1952) p. 312.

6. Meena Alexander, *Women in Romanticism* (Basingstoke and London: Macmillan, 1989) p. 147.

7. Mary Jacobus, *Romanticism, Writing and Sexual Difference* (Oxford: Clarendon Press, 1989) p. 251.

8. This ending was sketched out in a letter to George Smith, 10 December 1863. See J. A. V. Chapple, 'Elizabeth Gaskell: Two Unpublished Letters to George Smith', *Etudes Anglaises*, vol. 33 (1980) pp. 183–7.

9. For a discussion of Mrs Hamley as a model of feminine self-sacrifice who has a dangerous appeal for Molly, see Patricia Meyer Spacks, *The Female Imagination* (London: George Allen and Unwin, 1976) pp. 91–2.

10. Easson, *Elizabeth Gaskell*, p. 198.

11. Rich defines the 're-vision' she advocates for women writers and critics as 'the act of looking back, of seeing with fresh eyes, of entering an old text from a new critical direction'. See 'When We Dead Awaken: Writing as Re-Vision', in Adrienne Rich, *On Lies, Secrets and Silence: Selected Prose 1966–78* (London: Virago, 1980) p. 35.

Selected Bibliography

Works by Elizabeth Gaskell

Mary Barton (Harmondsworth: Penguin, 1970).
Cranford/Cousin Phillis (Harmondsworth: Penguin, 1976).
Ruth (Oxford: World's Classics, 1985).
North and South (Harmondsworth: Penguin, 1977).
The Life of Charlotte Brontë (Harmondsworth: Penguin, 1975).
My Lady Ludlow and Other Stories (Oxford: World's Classics, 1989).
Cousin Phillis and Other Tales (Oxford: World's Classics, 1981).
Sylvia's Lovers (Oxford: World's Classics, 1982).
Wives and Daughters (Oxford: World's Classics, 1987).
My Diary: The Early Years of my Daughter Marianne (London: privately printed by Clement Shorter, 1923).
The Letters of Mrs Gaskell, ed. J. A. V. Chapple and Arthur Pollard (Manchester: Manchester University Press, 1966).

Secondary Works

Alexander, Meena, *Women in Romanticism: Mary Wollstonecraft, Dorothy Wordsworth and Mary Shelley* (London: Macmillan, 1989).

Armstrong, Nancy, *Desire and Domestic Fiction: A Political History of the Novel* (Oxford: Oxford University Press, 1987).

Auerbach, Nina, *Communities of Women: An Idea in Fiction* (Cambridge, Mass.: Harvard University Press, 1978).

Basch, Françoise, *Relative Creatures: Victorian Women in Society and the Novel 1837–67*, trans. Anthony Rudolf (London: Allen Lane, 1974).

Benn, J. Miriam, 'Some Unpublished Gaskell Letters', *Notes and Queries*, vol. 225 (1980) pp. 507–15.

Bodenheimer, Rosemarie, '*North and South*: A Permanent State of Change', *Nineteenth-century Fiction*, vol. 34 (1979) pp. 281–301.

Bodenheimer, Rosemarie, 'Private Grief and Public Acts in

Mary Barton', *Dickens Studies Annual*, vol. 9 (1981) pp. 195–216.

Bodenheimer, Rosemarie, *The Politics of Story in Victorian Fiction* (Ithaca: Cornell University Press, 1988).

Brontë, Charlotte, *The Brontës: Their Lives, Friendships and Correspondence*, vol. IV: *1852–1928* (Oxford: Basil Blackwell, 1933).

Carlyle, Thomas, 'Corn Law Rhymes', in *Critical and Miscellaneous Essays*, vol. III (London: Chapman and Hall, 1899) pp. 136–66.

Carlyle, Thomas, 'Chartism', in *Critical and Miscellaneous Essays*, vol. IV (London: Chapman and Hall, 1899).

Carnall, Geoffrey, 'Dickens, Mrs Gaskell, and the Preston Strike', *Victorian Studies*, vol. 8 (1964-5) pp. 31–48.

Cazamian, Louis, *The Social Novel in England 1830–1850: Dickens, Disraeli, Mrs Gaskell, Kingsley*, trans. Martin Fido (London: Routledge and Kegan Paul, 1973).

Cecil, David, *Early Victorian Novelists: Essays in Revaluation* (London: Constable, 1934).

Chapple, J. A. V., 'Elizabeth Gaskell: Two Unpublished Letters to George Smith', *Etudes Anglaises*, vol. 33 (1980) pp. 183–7.

Craik, W. A., *Elizabeth Gaskell and the English Provincial Novel* (London: Methuen, 1975).

Crick, Brian, 'Mrs Gaskell's *Ruth*: A Reconsideration', *Mosaic*, vol. 9 (1977) no. 2, pp. 85–104.

Cunningham, Valentine, *Everywhere Spoken Against: Dissent in the Victorian Novel* (Oxford: Clarendon Press, 1975).

David, Deirdre, *Fictions of Resolution in Three Victorian Novels: North and South, Our Mutual Friend, Daniel Deronda* (New York: Columbia University Press, 1981).

David, Deirdre, *Intellectual Women and Victorian Patriarchy: Harriet Martineau, Elizabeth Barrett Browning, George Eliot* (London: Macmillan, 1987).

Dodsworth, Martin, 'Women Without Men at Cranford', *Essays in Criticism*, vol. 13 (1963) pp. 132–45.

Duthie, Enid L., *The Themes of Elizabeth Gaskell* (London: Macmillan, 1980).

Eagleton, Terry, '*Sylvia's Lovers* and Legality', *Essays in Criticism*, vol. 26 (1976) pp. 17–27.

Easson, Angus, *Elizabeth Gaskell* (London: Routledge and Kegan Paul, 1979).

Easson, Angus, 'Mr Hale's Doubts in *North and South*', *Review of English Studies*, vol. 31 (1980) pp. 30–40.

Foster, Shirley, *Victorian Women's Fiction: Marriage, Freedom and the Individual* (London: Croom Helm, 1985).

Fryckstedt, Monica Correa, *Elizabeth Gaskell's Mary Barton and Ruth: A Challenge to Christian England* (Uppsala: Almquist and Wiksell, 1982).

Furbank, P. N., 'Mendacity in Mrs Gaskell', *Encounter*, vol. 40 (1973) pp. 51–5.

Gallagher, Catherine, *The Industrial Reformation of English Fiction: Social Discourse and Narrative Form 1832–1867* (Chicago: Chicago University Press, 1985).

Ganz, Margaret, *Elizabeth Gaskell: The Artist in Conflict* (New York: Twayne, 1969).

Gérin, Winifred, *Elizabeth Gaskell: A Biography* (Oxford: Oxford University Press, 1980).

Haldane, Elizabeth, *Mrs Gaskell and Her Friends* (London: Hodder and Stoughton, 1931).

Harman, B. L., 'In Promiscuous Company: Female Public Appearance in Elizabeth Gaskell's *North and South*', *Victorian Studies*, vol. 31 (1988) pp. 351–74.

Helsinger, Elizabeth, Robin Lauterbach Sheets and William Veeder (eds), *The Woman Question: Society and Literature in Britain and America, 1837–1883*, 3 vols (New York: Garland, 1983).

Homans, Margaret, *Bearing the Word: Language and Female Experience in Nineteenth-century Women's Writing* (Chicago: Chicago University Press, 1986).

Hopkins, Annette B., *Elizabeth Gaskell: Her Life and Work* (London: John Lehmann, 1952).

Jackson, Rosemary, *Fantasy: The Literature of Subversion* (London: Methuen, 1981).

Jacobus, Mary, *Romanticism, Writing and Sexual Difference* (Oxford: Clarendon, 1989).

Jann, Rosemary, *The Art and Science of Victorian History* (Columbus: Ohio State University Press, 1985).

Lansbury, Coral, *Elizabeth Gaskell: The Novel of Social Crisis* (London: Paul Elek, 1975).

Lucas, John, 'Mrs Gaskell and Brotherhood', in David Howard, John Lucas and John Goode (eds), *Tradition and Tolerance in Nineteenth-century Fiction* (London: Routledge and Kegan Paul, 1966).

Lucas, John, 'Mrs Gaskell Reconsidered', *Victorian Studies*, vol. 11 (1967–8) pp. 528–33.

Lucas, John, *The Literature of Change: Studies in the Nineteenth-century Provincial Novel* (Brighton: Harvester, 1977).

[Ludlow, J. M.], 'Ruth: A Novel', *North British Review*, vol. 19 (1853) pp. 151–74.

Martin, C. A., 'Gaskell, Darwin and *North and South*', *Studies in the Novel*, vol. 15 (1983) pp. 91–107.

McVeagh, John, 'The Making of *Sylvia's Lovers*', *Modern Language Review*, vol. 65 (1970) pp. 272–81.

McVeagh, John, *Elizabeth Gaskell* (London: Routledge and Kegan Paul, 1970).

Morgan, Susan, *Sisters in Time: Imagining Gender in Nineteeth-century British Fiction* (New York and Oxford: Oxford University Press, 1989).

Nestor, Pauline, *Female Friendships and Communities: Charlotte Brontë, George Eliot, Elizabeth Gaskell* (Oxford: Clarendon Press, 1985).

Owens, Craig, 'The Discourse of Others: Feminists and Postmodernism', in Hal Foster (ed.), *Postmodern Culture* (London: Pluto Press, 1985).

Rance, Nicholas, *The Historical Novel and Popular Politics in Nineteenth-century England* (London: Vision Press, 1975).

Rignall, J. M., 'The Historical Double: *Waverley, Sylvia's Lovers, The Trumpet-Major*', *Essays in Criticism*, vol. 34 (1984) pp. 14–32.

Rubenius, Aina, *The Woman Question in Mrs Gaskell's Life and Work* (Uppsala, 1950).

Ruskin, John, *Sesame and Lilies* (1865; London: George Allen, 1901).

Sanders, Andrew, *The Victorian Historical Novel 1840–1880* (London: Macmillan, 1978).

Sharps, J. G., *Mrs Gaskell's Observation and Invention: A Study of her Non-biographic Works* (Sussex: Linden Press, 1970).

Shelston, A. J., 'Ruth, Mrs Gaskell's Neglected Novel', *Bulletin of the John Rylands Library*, vol. 58 (1975) pp. 173–92.

Stone, Donald D., *The Romantic Impulse in Victorian Fiction* (Cambridge, Mass.: Harvard University Press, 1980).

Stoneman, Patsy, *Elizabeth Gaskell* (Brighton: Harvester, 1987).

[Taylor, Harriet], 'Enfranchisement of Women', *Westminster Review*, vol. 55 (1851) pp. 289–311.

Vicinus, Martha, *Suffer and Be Still: Women in the Victorian Age* (Bloomington: Indiana University Press, 1972).

Vicinus, Martha, *The Industrial Muse: A Study of Nine-teenth-century British Working-class Literature* (London: Croom Helm, 1974).

Weiss, Barbara, 'Elizabeth Gaskell: The Telling of Feminine Tales', *Studies in the Novel*, vol. 16 (1984) pp. 274–87.

Wilbur, Earl Morse, *A History of Unitarianism: Socianism and Its Antecedents* (Cambridge, Mass.: Harvard University Press, 1946).

Wilbur, Earl Morse, *A History of Unitarianism in Transylvania, England and America* (Cambridge, Mass.: Harvard University Press, 1952).

Williams, Raymond, *Culture and Society 1780–1950* (1958; Harmondsworth: Penguin, 1971).

Woolf, Virginia, *A Room of One's Own* (St Albans: Panther, 1977).

Wright, Edgar, *Mrs Gaskell: The Basis for Reassessment* (London: Oxford University Press, 1965).

Yeazell, Ruth, 'Why Political Novels have Heroines: *Sybil, Mary Barton* and *Felix Holt*', *Novel*, vol. 18 (1985) pp. 126–44.

Index